how to survive as a Good Church School

A guide for all governors of Church of England and Church in Wales schools

C000271918

CONTENTS

FOREWORD

It is a truth universally acknowledged that we live in times of great uncertainty and upheaval for education in England and Wales. For better or worse, almost every aspect of the ways our schools are governed, owned, resourced and run seems to be up for grabs. As Christians react to change, it is important to remember that there have been church schools for over a thousand years, and that they have weathered many storms, adapting and evolving to survive and flourish.

The years since the Second World War were shaped by a single primary statute, R.A. Butler's 1944 Education Act. This secured a school system that was nationally provided but locally delivered, within which state schools were either aided or controlled by churches. Now, after thirty years of chipping away, the settled order of school organisation Butler established is scheduled for the scrapyard.

Whether we like the politics of this or not, one consequence of academisation, with all its challenges and opportunities, is a crying need for able and fully committed governors and trustees. Increasingly people of goodwill in the community need to be willing and able to exercise the kind of headline responsibility that once lay with local government. This book is a resource to help new recruits to church school governance understand how they can do this intelligently and effectively. That said, it is also for seasoned school governors because, as the role is reinvented and the scenery shifts, there is a danger that what they think they know will turn out to be wrong and lead good people into bad mistakes.

Some church school educators will look back on the Butler years with warmth and affection. The fact is, however, that they are lost and gone for ever, and it is important that church school governors, while aware of our rich and resourceful heritage, do not end up like Colonel Redfern in John Osborne's *Look Back in Anger*, whom Jimmy describes as "just one of those sturdy plants left over from the Edwardian Wilderness that can't understand why the sun isn't shining any more".

By way of contrast, Jesus taught his disciples to be ever watchful. He sent them out into the world's uncertainty and upheaval as sheep among wolves with a charge to be "wise as serpents and innocent as doves". Never was that advice more relevant to anyone than it is for Christian educators today. As radical policy shifts break on the scene, governing bodies need to be well-informed, self-aware and able. The enhanced powers assumed by the Secretary of State since 2010 are largely, since 2014, wielded by newly-appointed Regional Schools Commissioners, with whom good relationships must be built. Building and running Multi-Academy Trusts requires imaginative partnership with a potentially bewildering variety of other schools, trusts and bodies. Church schools have to build good relationships with new partners and chart a course that retains the social, spiritual and academic welfare of our children, parents and staff as their main aim. Their biggest resource in doing this is the school's Christian ethos.

Christian communities set the Good Shepherd at their hearts. They are called to work intentionally to make themselves places where everybody is somebody. One particular concern for governors has to be securing and sustaining the school as a safe and caring community. As well as safeguarding, dignity at work and anti-bullying policies, governors need to make sure schools excel in equality and diversity. Above all, governors need to build mutual trust all round. There is an old equation that says that Trust = Credibility + Reliability + Relationship, divided by Perception of Self-interest.

As all the waymarks shift, Christian educators need to be spiritually grounded people whose hearts are fixed where lasting joys are to be found, but who are also prepared to think and do radical things, sometimes with new partners, for the good of the children and society they serve.

The real challenge of being a governor in a church school is two-fold. Firstly, governors are keepers of the flame. They take responsibility for the most important foundational aspect of school life – the Christian ethos and character one former secretary of state famously wished could be bottled and handed out over the counter to all schools. All governors, not just those representing the foundation, are there to understand and articulate the school's values and standards, and secure maximum alignment with them. This will involve understanding and following up SIAMS inspections, and making sure the school relates to its foundation as a church school, not only by having the fact on its letterhead, but in Spirit and truth. This includes promoting mutually enriching relationships with the actual church community whose name is painted on the school noticeboard. It will also involve working to build strong and harmonious relationships between foundation and other members of the governing body.

Secondly, governors have to be intentionally competent and add real value to the life of the school, respecting the difference between governance and management. Wise governors in every institution know that although the occasional emergency may require a blue-light response, their usual mode has to be "eyes open and hands off". Fuzziness on this point destabilises the school by undermining and demotivating good staff. What they have to do is work hard, not only to climb the mountain of paperwork, but to discern and offer, from the fullness of their hearts and minds, what they can bring to the school that, all things considered, adds genuine value to it.

This book explores how this difficult, if not impossible, two-fold vocation can be fulfilled honestly, competently and even, surprisingly often perhaps, with joy.

The Rt Revd Dr Alan Wilson
Bishop of Buckingham and Chair, Oxford Diocesan Board of Education

INTRODUCTION

*H*ow to Survive as a Governor of a Church School aims to help ALL governors, whether new or experienced, coming from a church-based background or none. The aim is to provide you with the knowledge, practical skills and confidence to enable you to serve the school of which you are a governor or considering becoming a governor. This in turn should enable the school, its staff and students to achieve their full potential:

- In religious terms – to engage with and live out Christian values, wherever and in whatever situation they find themselves.

- In educational terms, whatever the level of achievement.

- As adults and full members of society.

So is this book just for foundation governors?
No. This book is for everyone who is part of a board or governing body of a Church of England (C of E) or Church in Wales (C in W) school. The focus of the book is the state-funded compulsory sector.

Is this book written for committed Christians only?
No again. While many governors may well be regular worshipping members in the Church of England or Church in Wales, others will be members of another Christian denomination or of no religious affiliation. This book is written from a Christian perspective, however, and as a governor or prospective governor of a church school, it is strongly recommended that you think about and engage with the Christian faith – the cornerstone upon which the school is founded and run.

Reflection

Just take a moment to think. What is your personal view on the Christian faith, the Christian Church and the central figure of Jesus Christ? Are there any "stumbling blocks" or worries that prevent you from fulfilling the role to the best of your potential? If so, the best way forward is to air and discuss them in whatever way you think most appropriate – be that with other governors, a friend or member of the clergy.

A tool for developing the individual governor and the governing body

Throughout the book we have included questions and exercises for you to work through – both as an individual and as a governing body. We hope that the book will be flexible enough to accommodate all local circumstances and needs. It may be that, at your first meeting of the new academic year as a governing body, you include an agenda item on the best way to use it.

Each chapter has been designed to enable you to develop and grow in your role and understand the various challenges and constraints that all those involved in C of E or C in W school education face:

- *Chapter One* focuses on the landscape of C in W and C of E schools – how we arrived and where we are now.

- *Chapter Two* looks at how as governors you are guardians of the vision, tasked with turning that vision into a workable mission.

- *Chapter Three* can be used as a resource for the individual governor, or for anyone wanting to know how to go about the induction, review and self-evaluation of a governor.

- *Chapter Four* addresses some of the more common challenges, with some practical suggestions and solutions.

- *Chapter Five* looks at how important it is for a governing body to have a robust system of ongoing self-evaluation and review in place, and offers some suggestions.

- *Chapter Six* discusses what every governor dreads – the school inspection. In particular, it looks at the requirements of the Statutory Inspection of Anglican and Methodist Schools (SIAMS, Section 48) and the Gwella (Section 50) inspections, and considers how best to prepare for inspection.

- *Chapter Seven* offers some resources for governor meetings and individual spirituality.

Governors are busy people, so this is designed to be a book that can either be read cover to cover, or one that can be dipped into. Each chapter is self-contained and can be read on its own. Some sections may be particularly relevant to your role and circumstances, while others are less so. However you come to and use it, we hope that it will be a companion on your journey as a governor.

CHAPTER 1

A LOOK AT THE LANDSCAPE:
Church schools in England and Wales

What are church schools?

Inclusive schools for the community

Church of England (C of E) and Church in Wales (C in W) schools exist and are run primarily for the communities in which they are located. As the Church of England website puts it: "They are inclusive and serve equally those who are of the Christian faith, those of other faiths and those with no faith,"[1] while the Church in Wales website states that: "Our schools are inclusive by nature, serving children and young people in a range of communities. They also form a natural point of community focus, whether in the inner city or in rural villages."[2]

Equally, governors of church schools are representative of the communities in which they are located – be they foundation,[3] community, parent, local authority or staff governors. Like the students and staff, a member of the governing body may be a member of a Christian denomination other than the C of E or C in W, or of another religion, or indeed of no religious affiliation.[4]

The reach of church schools in state education

Church schools in England and Wales are key providers of education at primary, secondary and tertiary levels. In the state sector the C of E and the C in W are important partner providers with local authorities in compulsory education. Over five hundred independent schools declare themselves in their trust deeds, mission statements or other documents to be Anglican in ethos.[5]

The C of E and C in W are also important players in the post-compulsory and private education sectors, with a presence in many further and higher education institutes and a number of higher education institutions having an explicitly Anglican foundation.[6] However, it is the state-funded compulsory sector where our focus lies.

A few statistics[7]

- Approximately 1 million children attend C of E schools and 25,000 children C in W schools.

- About 15 million people alive today went to a C of E school.

- There are 4,500 C of E primary schools and over 200 C of E secondary schools.

- There are 172 C in W primary and secondary schools, supporting the careers of over 5,000 teachers and support staff.

- With more than 130 sponsored and 350 converter academies,[8] the Church is the biggest sponsor of academies in England. (There are no academies in Wales.)

- In the C of E alone, clergy dedicate an estimated million hours every year to working with children and young people in schools, often providing holiday and after-school activities.

- There are 22,500 foundation governors in C of E schools – recruited, trained and supported by dioceses.

Church schools in England and Wales have a long-standing and distinguished place in the national education picture. Many would say that the Church had and has a pivotal role in establishing the principle of education for all that we take for granted in the UK today. In a House of Lords speech in 2011, Lord Hill of Oareford summed it up: "It is difficult to dissociate from the history of the country the role that the Church has played over a long period in individual schools and also collectively in society."[9]

How church schools began – a historical overview

The first church school in Great Britain is reckoned to be King's School in Canterbury, founded by Augustine in AD 597. Throughout the fifteenth, sixteenth and seventeenth centuries, choir schools were founded to educate choristers and "deserving poor" children. Alongside that was what could be termed the "charity school movement", with Christ's Hospital, the first Bluecoats school (after its distinctive uniform), founded in 1552.

Griffith Jones and the Welsh Circulating Schools

Griffith Jones (1684-1761)

Griffith Jones was born in 1683 or 1684 at Penboyr in Carmarthenshire. He was ordained in 1708 and appointed rector of Llanddowror in 1716, where he remained for the rest of his life. In 1731 he established the first Circulating School, in order to teach people to read. The name came from the fact that the schools were established and run for a brief period by itinerant teachers, who would then move on, having trained local teachers. Lessons were in Welsh, and the emphasis was on teaching basic literacy using religious texts provided by the Society for Promoting Christian Knowledge (SPCK – still a flourishing organisation and publishing house today). Teaching took place in a variety of buildings, including in one case a windmill. The National Society established schools in Wales and England, and by 1833, when the government began to contribute to the funding of education, there were 146 Anglican church schools in Wales, as opposed to only fifteen in England. It is estimated that over two hundred thousand people learnt to read in the Circulating Schools, and that by the time of Griffith Jones' death in 1761 there were 3,500 such schools.

One key difference between Wales and England was (and remains) the strength of Welsh Nonconformist denominations, with some parents refusing to send their children to Anglican schools. The Church in Wales Act passed in 1916, but not implemented until 1920, disestablished the Anglican Church in Wales. State government devolution in 1999 reinforced the separation of education policy and management between England and Wales.

Some key dates in Welsh education[10]

1699 – inaugural meeting of the Society for Promoting Christian Knowledge (SPCK).

1731 – Griffith Jones of Penboyr in Dyfed sets up the first Circulating School.

1811 – foundation of the National Society for the Education of the Poor in the Principles of the Established Church.

1833 – the National Society starts to receive an annual subsidy to establish schools. At this point there are 147 C in W schools in existence.

1843 – a bill is introduced to establish (state) schools for the children of the poor. It fails due to protests by Nonconformists against the Anglican domination on proposed school boards.

1847 – publication of *The Treachery of the Blue Books*, a report which recognises the religious and class divides which have hampered the progress of education in Wales.

1870 – the Elementary Education Act establishes the framework for schooling of all children between the ages of 5 and 13.

1905 – the Coercion of Wales Act provides for local authority (county council) control over C in W schools and an end to religious tests for teachers. The Liberal government which comes to power in December withdraws the Act.

1916 – the disestablishment of the Anglican Church in Wales. It is not implemented until 1920.

1944 – the Education Act makes all schooling free for all pupils and raises the school leaving age to 15.

1945 – the Model Articles sets out the duties of school governors.

1965 – the largest expansion of comprehensive schools takes place.

1985 – the Swann Report, *Education for All*, strongly recommends a pluralist approach to religious education.

1988 – the Education Reform Act establishes the National Curriculum and gives parents the right to choose which school their child should attend, or whether to home educate them instead.

Joshua Watson and the National Society

Much of what we know today is a result of the vision of Joshua Watson, the founder of the National Society.

Joshua Watson
(1771–1855)

Joshua Watson was born in 1771 in Tower Hill, London. He was the second son of John Watson, who rose from humble beginnings to become a wealthy wine merchant and government contractor. Joshua's elder brother John went into the Church, becoming first Rector of St John's Church, Hackney and then Archdeacon of St Albans. Joshua was sent to be an apprentice in book-keeping in preparation for entering his father's business. This motivated him to aspire to greater things, and by the age of forty-three he was sufficiently wealthy to retire from business in order to concentrate on other matters.

Joshua and his brother were part of a close group of friends, who belonged to the "high church" movement – so called because they held the Church and the sacraments in high regard. In 1811 this group – known as the Hackney Phalanx – founded the National Society for the Education of the Poor in the Principles of the Established Church. It was initially conceived as a branch of the SPCK.

The establishment of the National Society consolidated the Church's place in the education-for-all movement. The Archbishop of Canterbury, Charles Manners-Sutton, chaired the National Society's inaugural meeting and became its first president. At a time when education for all was held to be politically dangerous, the aim of the National Society was to raise money by voluntary subscription to support the provision of a church school in every parish in England. Its stated purpose was that:

National Religion should be made the foundation of National Education, and should be the first and chief thing taught to the Poor, according to the excellent Liturgy and Catechism provided by our Church.[11]

With regard to children, the National Society's objectives were:

… to teach them the doctrine of Religion according to the principles of the Established Church, and to train them to the performance of their religious duties by an early discipline [and] to communicate such knowledge and habits as are sufficient though life in their proper station. [12]

The reference to "their proper station" might sound odd these days, but in the early nineteenth century this was a radical proposition. Hannah More (1745-1833), a pioneer of church schools in Somerset, stated that no system of education for the poor should: "pass the bounds of their condition in society". She reasoned that: "To give men ambitions that could not be fulfilled, aspirations that could not be met, was to make men unhappy and society unstable." [13]

The National Society's educational objective was primarily religious instruction, but also general education in literacy and numeracy, to enable children from poor families to achieve their potential and escape the routine of child labour that was all too familiar in the mid-nineteenth century. [14]

The Sunday School movement
Driving forward the Church's role in making education for school-aged children universally available regardless of socio-economic group or income was Robert Raikes (1736-1811), generally regarded as the founder of the Sunday School

movement. As well as teaching scripture, Sunday Schools taught basic literacy to make the Bible and the Book of Common Prayer accessible, as well as to balance sacred and secular learning.

Underlying the Sunday School movement and the foundation of the National Society was the increasing realisation during the nineteenth century that child labour – in mines, mills and factories – was a moral scandal which deprived children of even a basic education.

Church and state in education
A major step forward in the educational partnership between Church and state took place in 1833, when the Whig (Liberal) government voted to award the National Society an annual subsidy to help in the establishment of schools. From then on the provision of education for all, regardless of income or class, grew exponentially. This was consolidated in the 1944 Education Act.

During the 1950s, 1960s and 1970s, the debate around religious education shifted, as waves of migration to the UK created a far more multicultural, ethnically diverse society. Inevitably, questions started to be asked about whether children in schools should learn about other faiths as well as Christianity. It is a debate that continues to this day, and will doubtless crop up in your role as a governor. Perhaps because of this, and because of the introduction of the comprehensive school system, which sought to standardise education, it's fair to say that these decades were characterised by a shift away from faith-based education.

That trend started to be reversed in the late 1980s, when the emphasis moved away from "one-size-fits-all" education and greater parental choice was introduced. In 2001 a government Green Paper, *Schools: Building on Success*, made a commitment to "autonomy and diversity":

We want a secondary school system in which… Every school has a distinct mission, ethos and character, and the autonomy to manage its own affairs provided it demonstrates success. [15]

The paper recognised the value of faith-based schools and suggested a collaborative procedure for enabling community schools to become church schools through partnership with local education authorities, where there is local agreement.

In response, the Church Schools Review Group, chaired by Lord Dearing, published a report welcoming the Green Paper and concluding that the Church of England "has probably its best opportunity in education since the 1944 Education Act". It also recognised that responding to the opportunity represented a major challenge for the Church. [16]

Thirteenth-century mosaic of Jesus Christ in the Hagia Sophia temple in Istanbul, Turkey

Some key dates in England

597 – foundation of the King's School, Canterbury – reputed to be the oldest school in England.

1699 – inaugural meeting of the Society for Promoting Christian Knowledge (SPCK).

1703 – Old Schools Trust (now the Church Schools of Cambridge) founded by the Revd William Whiston "to train poor children in the knowledge of God, and in the Christian Religion".[17]

1780 – the Sunday School movement, pioneered by Robert Raikes, is established as a national movement.

1811 – foundation of the National Society for the Education of the Poor in the Principles of the Established Church.

1830 – the Sunday School Union is formed – over 7,000 Sunday schools with 9,000 teachers and 845,000 pupils.[18]

1833 – the National Society starts to receive an annual subsidy to establish schools.

1870 – the Elementary Education Act establishes the framework for schooling of all children between the ages of 5 and 13.

1944 – the Education Act makes all schooling free for all pupils and raises the school leaving age to 15.

1945 – the Model Articles set out the duties of school governors.

1965 – the largest expansion of comprehensive schools takes place.

1985 – the Swann Report, *Education for All*, strongly recommends a pluralist approach to religious education.

1988 – the Education Reform Act establishes the National Curriculum and gives parents the right to choose which school their child should attend, or whether to home educate them instead.

2001 – the Dearing Report, *The Way Ahead*, is published in response to the government Green Paper, *Schools: Building on Success*.

2012 – *The Church School of the Future*, known as the Chadwick Report, is published.

Key bodies working with church schools today

The National Society

The National Society continues to exist to this day. It is based at Church House in Westminster with the other National Church Institutions (NCIs) under the overall umbrella of the Archbishops' Council.[19] It works closely with the wider Education Office of the Church of England and with the Church in Wales Education Officer, and is responsible for:

- Negotiating with the government and other national agencies to maintain and develop the contribution of church schools to public education in England and Wales.

- Supporting and advising diocesan education teams on legal and technical, curriculum and ethos issues.

- Contributing a Christian perspective to the national education debate.

Together with the Board of Education, the National Society collaborates with the Catholic Education Service and the Methodist Church, along with other Christian and faith education representatives, to ensure that the needs of faith communities are represented in the national debate.[20]

Church in Wales Governing Body

In Wales, education services are run at a diocesan level and are answerable to the Church in Wales Governing Body. The Governing Body is the supreme legislature of the Church in Wales. It is responsible for decisions that affect the Church's faith, order and worship. It also has powers to make regulations "for the general management and good government of the Church, and the property and affairs thereof".[21]

The Church of England Education Office and the National Society

The Church of England Education Office serves children and adults in a variety of church and educational settings and seeks to promote an education that allows children and young people to live out Jesus' promise of life in all its fullness.

Providing support within an operating framework between the Archbishops' Council and the National Society, the Education Office works with the Diocesan Boards of Education and oversees the administration of the Statutory Inspection of Anglican and Methodist Schools (SIAMS).[22]

Some questions

- Do you know who your General Synod members are?

- Do you know how to instigate a debate about education policy in the Church of England or Church in Wales?

Diocesan Boards of Education in England and Wales

Each diocese in the C of E and the C in W has a Diocesan Board of Education (DBE), which drives policy and ensures that national church school policy is implemented locally. Much of the direction will be guided by the General Synod in England and the Governing Body in Wales, and the respective Houses of Bishops, although the emphasis is always on local needs and situations. Your diocese will provide training programmes and resources which are tailored to your particular area and requirements.

Action points

Find out:

- Who the Diocesan Director of Education is in your diocese.

- The DBE training programme for the coming academic year.

- What other resources and support are available through the DBE.

Organisational aspects of C of E and C in W schools

C of E and C in W schools fall into a number of categories. There are various nuances of groupings. For governors, the category of school has a direct influence on:

- The way in which it is governed.

- The way in which staff are appointed (this is a key responsibility of the governing body).

- The ownership and control of capital assets, such as property and land.

- The curriculum to be followed.

The differences are summarised in the table below (for more detailed guidance consult your DBE).[23]

Category of school	Make-up of governing body	Ownership of capital assets	Staff appointments	Curriculum	Legal status	Approx. number in England & Wales
Voluntary Aided (VA)	Foundation governors outnumber other governors	Charity, religious group or governing body (usually the DBE)	Made by governing body	National Curriculum	Maintained	1,891
Voluntary Controlled (VC)	Local authority governors in the majority; potentially only 2 or 3 foundation governors	Local authority	Made by local authority	National Curriculum	Maintained	2,255
Academy	According to the trust deed	Charity, religious group or governing body (usually the DBE)	Made by governing body	Can determine own curriculum	Academy	575
Foundation school	According to the trust deed	Charity, religious group or governing body (usually the DBE)	Made by governing body	Can determine own curriculum	Academy	34

There is a considerable amount of local variation regarding the detailed arrangements for allocation of places on the governing body and appointment of governors – the DBE or clerk to the governors should have the details for any individual school.

Academy or not?

In recent years the government has been very keen to encourage schools to become academies. For any school it is a major step, driven by the governing body. In-depth consultation needs to take place, with key stakeholders sounded out. The educational, financial and practical aspects of making the change need to be considered, and questions about the ownership and control of any property, land or other assets must be resolved. For church schools, governors additionally need to consider how becoming an academy could potentially affect a school's ethos and religious focus. Several dioceses have established Multi-Academy Trusts (MATs) to support schools that do decide to go down the academy route.

The appointment and role of foundation governors

Foundation governors are unique to schools that have a religious or historic foundation, such as church schools. They represent the C of E or C in W on the governing body and are a vital link between the school and the wider worshipping community. This is in addition to the statutory responsibilities held by all governors.

The National Society stated in 1996 that foundation governors are there to, "explore, with their partners on the Governing Body, ways in which the Church's role in the school may be more fully and positively implemented".[24]

Generally, the incumbent or another member of the clergy will be an ex officio member of the governing body, but need not be the chair. In most dioceses the appointment of other foundation governors is the responsibility of the Parochial Church Council (PCC), although this may be delegated to a sub-committee or directly to the incumbent.

The criteria that a foundation governor candidate or appointee should fulfil are:

- Understanding the distinctive nature and history of C of E or C in W schools.

- Being sympathetic to the needs of all members of the school community, including pupils, staff and other governors and partners, such as the local authority.

- An ability to attend governors' full meetings, sub-committees and visit the school informally.

- Willingness to undertake appropriate governor training.

- An ability to build relationships between the school and the parish.

- Being a regular attender at their (preferably but not necessarily) Anglican place of worship. A PCC may decide that, if a candidate is strong in particular areas required by the governing body and a regular worshipping member in another Christian denomination, they would be a suitable appointment.

Governors, PCCs and DBEs should all be wary of making nominations or appointments just because someone seems vaguely suitable. It is much more important to find a candidate who has the necessary background, confidence and financial knowledge to challenge an inadequate headteacher, for example, or to question why educational standards in the school are not higher, or to speak up when the school's Christian values are not being fully or properly upheld.

How church schools perform in the educational landscape

C of E and C in W schools have a long and highly respected heritage. The supporting bodies – the National Society, the Church of England Education Office, and in particular the DBEs – are pivotal in ensuring that children are educated to the highest standards, that appropriate staff are appointed, and that leadership teams are fully robust and answerable to parents, staff and wider bodies.

audioscience / Shutterstock.com

Some figures

- 84% of C of E primary schools are rated "Good" or "Outstanding" by Ofsted, compared to 81% of non-C of E schools.

- 75% of C of E secondary schools are rated "Good" or "Outstanding" by Ofsted, compared to 71% of non-C of E schools.

- 92% of C of E primary schools and 90% of C of E secondary schools are rated "Good" or "Outstanding" under the SIAMS inspection framework, which assesses levels of spiritual and pastoral support.[25]

In terms of inclusiveness, C of E schools are broadly in line with national averages:

- 15% of C of E pupils are eligible for free school meals, in line with the national average.

- 25% of C of E pupils are from ethnic minority backgrounds, just 1% below the national average of 26%.[26]

As we have seen, church schools have a rich history in the provision of education for all in both England and Wales. This ethos of universal access to education free at the point of delivery which has inclusiveness at its heart is paramount in the way that C of E and C in W schools are managed. As a governor, you are instrumental in carrying forward the vision of Joshua Watson, albeit in a very different world from that of 250 years ago. So it's a good idea to take some time to reflect on and pray about this and consider where you as a governor figure in this landscape and how you can continue the tradition and carry it forward.

Personal reflection

- Why was I asked to be a governor?

- If asked for suggestions on who could join our governing body, who would I recommend and why?

- How can I be sure they are suitable?

- What can I learn from this person's qualities that can inform the work I do as a governor?

ENDNOTES

[1] The Church of England/Education & National Society/Church Schools and Academies: www.churchofengland.org

[2] The Church in Wales/Schools/Education: www.churchinwales.org.uk

[3] You can find out more about the role of foundation governors on page 16. See also: Church of England, Archbishops' Council Education Division & the National Society, Importance of Foundation Governors (2013), at: www.churchofengland.org/media/1397450/importanceoffoundationgovernors.pdf

[4] Every school governor must be a UK citizen over the age of eighteen, who is not disqualified under the School Governance (Constitution) (England) Regulations of 2012.

[5] The Woodard Foundation: www.woodard.co.uk

[6] The Church of England/Education/Colleges and Universities: www.churchofengland.org

[7] Figures from the Church of England/Education: www.churchofengland.org; & the Church in Wales/Life/Schools: www.churchinwales.org.uk

[8] Schools that were previously maintained and have voluntarily converted to academy status.

[9] Quoted by Tim Elbourne in Understanding Church Schools: Ideas for Today from Joshua Watson's Founding Vision (Cambridge: Grove Booklets, 2012), 5.

[10] Powys Heritage Online: http://history.powys.org.uk/history/common/educ1.html

[11] The Christian Remembrancer, vol. I (F.C. & J. Rivington, 1819).

[12] Quoted in David Blundell, Education and Construction of Childhood (London: Continuum, 2012).

[13] P. Hollis, The Pauper Press: A Study in Working-class Radicalism of the 1830s (Oxford: OUP, 1970), 5.

[14] Tim Elbourne, Understanding Church Schools: Ideas for Today from Joshua Watson's Founding Vision (Cambridge: Grove Booklets, 2012).

[15] Department for Education and Employment, Schools: Building on Success (Norwich: HMSO, 2001).

[16] The Archbishops' Council, The Way Ahead: Church of England Schools in the New Millennium (London: Church House Publishing, 2001).

[17] The Church Schools of Cambridge: www.csoc.org.uk/history

[18] H. Burgess, Enterprise in Education (London: SPCK, 1958), 13.

[19] The Church of England/About Us/Structure/The Archbishops' Council: www.churchofengland.org

[20] The Church of England/Education & National Society/Church Schools and Academies/National Society: www.churchofengland.org

[21] The Church in Wales/Structure/Governing Body: www.churchinwales.org.uk

[22] The Church of England/Education & National Society: www.churchofengland.org/education

[23] New Schools Network, Comparison of Different Types of School: A Guide to Schools in England, January 2015: www.newschoolsnetwork.org.

[24] Oxford Diocesan Board of Education Foundation, Foundation Governors: A Guide for Clergy: www.oxford.anglican.org

[25] Ofsted Summary of Latest Judgements, accurate as of 31 March 2014: www.churchofengland.org/education.aspx

[26] Department for Education, 2013 School Census: www.churchofengland.org/education.aspx

Q & A with the Archbishop of Wales, Dr Barry Morgan, at Peterston Super Ely C in W Primary School

CHAPTER 2

GUARDIANS OF THE VISION: What vision and mission mean for governors of church schools

On Jesus' arrival in heaven, a vast host of angels greeted him. After the formalities, they asked whom he had left behind on earth to finish the work he had begun.

Jesus replied, "Just a small group of men and women who love me."

"That's all?" asked the angels, astonished. "What if this tiny group should fail?"

Jesus replied, "I have no other plans."

(Author unknown)

What makes a Church of England (C of E) or Church in Wales (C in W) school different, and so by extension why should a parent want to send their child there, or a teacher want to teach there? And, of course, why would a governor want to be a governor there?

Apart from some organisational, administrative and regulatory differences, what makes a church school distinctive from a secular one can be surprisingly difficult to articulate, but perhaps it is best summed up as "vision". As guardians of the vision, governors are keeping alive the vision that was entrusted to that small group of men and women of the early Church.

In this chapter we will take a broader look at what is meant by "vision", how a school's vision is implemented as its mission, and how both vision and mission are underpinned by its values and ethos. There will be suggestions as to how you can reflect on what those terms mean for you as a governor and how, whether or not you identify as a practising Christian or member of the C of E or C in W, you can engage with the vision of the school you serve.

A continuity of vision

Joshua Watson's original vision

Joshua Watson's personal values, and by extension those of the movements and projects with which he was associated, were above all being true to God's work – whatever was appropriate in the local circumstance that would further the work of God was seen as a Christian value.

Watson was also motivated by a concern for the poor – not from a paternalistic perspective, but stemming from the New Testament teaching on the Christian duty to the poor (for example, in Luke 14:12-14 and Matthew 19:21). The key part that C of E and C in W schools play in areas of profound poverty is a tribute to Watson's perseverance in this.

You will be blessed, because they cannot repay you.

(Luke 14:14)

Watson has often been described as an "internationalist", in that he had a concern for the Anglican Communion and people overseas. The place of C of E and C in W schools in areas with a high ethnic minority population reflects and continues Watson's vision of truly inclusive education.

A further aspect of how Watson lived his life was hospitality. He made his Westminster house a place of welcome, both to social visitors and to longer-staying guests. Welcoming, including and valuing the contribution of people from all backgrounds and traditions should be a key aspect of C of E and C in W schools – reinforcing their ethos of being community schools, as opposed to admitting only those from any particular denomination or religion.

"You shall love the Lord your God with all your heart, and with all your soul, and with all your mind." This is the greatest and first commandment. And a second is like it: "You shall love your neighbour as yourself." On these two commandments hang all the law and the prophets.

(Matthew 22:37-40)

The vision today

The National Society's vision and values

The National Society's website outlines no fewer than fifteen values for schools, which exemplify the Christian faith. These are: reverence, wisdom, thankfulness, humility, endurance, service, compassion, trust, peace, forgiveness, friendship, justice, hope, creation and *koinonia* (from the Greek meaning communion or participation).[1] Although many of these are not exclusively Christian, they can all be described and framed in a distinctively Christian way.

Tip

Why not make one of these values the subject of your collective worship, PSHE (personal, social, health and economic) activities or personal reflection? You could focus on a different one each day, week, month or half term.

Author and educationalist **Neville Norcross** suggests five core values: hope, justice, humility, service, love. He suggests that vision and values are often confused, but in fact are different and distinct – that living the values and enabling them to permeate every aspect of school life is key, and that leaders (in this case governors) should lead by example.[2]

Tim Elbourne, also an author and educationalist, takes a step back from the multitude of values and characterises them according to the concepts they represent. He suggests: belonging, rootedness and narrative as core ideas which are given practical manifestations in the National Society's fifteen values.

Belonging, rootedness, narrative

- *Belonging* in this sense refers to community and relationship. Schools are communities in which relationships are formed, but also part of wider communities – the parish, the diocese, the Church as a whole, the local and wider secular communities.

- *Rootedness* articulates the idea that C of E and C in W schools have their roots in the Gospel. Strong roots lead to a flourishing life and enable growth for individuals and communities. They also help when enduring periods of testing and struggle.

- *Narrative* refers to salvation history – God working through his people, as told in the Old and New Testaments. This, Elbourne suggests, should be played out in every aspect of school life – formal lessons, collective worship, in the way that school life as a whole is conducted by children and young people, staff, parents, and of course governors.[3]

A project to establish strengths and weaknesses in your school's vision

- Find out whether your Diocesan Board of Education (DBE) has its own set of values for schools.

- Using one of the frameworks above and/or the DBE framework, brainstorm ways in which your school is strong and weak in each of the values identified. (You could organise a governors' "away day", to really give this the attention it warrants.)

- Provide evidence of the strengths (this will be important in any inspection[4]) and consider ways in which areas of weakness can be improved.

- Create an action plan to maintain the strengths and turn the weaknesses into strengths.

Guardians of the vision

As Joshua Watson realised two hundred and fifty years ago, schools are key shapers of society. This means that the role of the governor as a guardian of the vision has never been more important than it is today. So what does being a "guardian of the vision" mean for a governor of a church school? And what does it mean for you?

The word "vision" implies an affinity with the aims and values of the school that goes far beyond agreeing with a school's educational or business strategy, or approving its administrative procedures. This is about the bigger picture – the real reason why any of us bothers with any of it.

Let's take as our starting point the vision statements of a variety of church schools:

Some examples of vision statements in church schools

"To be a dynamic community of care, built on Christian values, in which everyone is encouraged, challenged and inspired."

"As a church school, at the heart of the community in partnership with parents, XXX CE Primary School is committed to enabling all pupils to achieve their full potential. We will do this through developing a love of learning within a creative environment, where everyone aspires towards excellence."

"We aim to provide a quality of education, within a safe, stimulating Christian environment."

"We aim to provide and welcome opportunities to prepare our children for their roles as members of an intercultural and multi-faith community."

An exercise

Take these and any other vision statements you can find and spend some time – either as an individual or with other governors, staff, or children and young people – reflecting on how they apply – or not – to your school. For example, is your school "a dynamic community of care" and a "safe, stimulating Christian environment"? Does that articulate what you aspire to, or would you want to phrase it differently? How does your school's own vision statement reflect reality?

When you take a close look at these vision statements, they are ambitious and may seem unachievable in, for example, a school where morale is low after a poor inspection, or where differences among the governors threatens to undermine consensus. At such times, to be the guardian of a vision might seem a particularly daunting challenge – but nevertheless, that is what governors are mandated to do. Moreover, staying true to the vision will, guaranteed, ultimately enable you to turn things around.

In reality, there are probably numerous reasons why you are a governor, or are considering becoming one. Perhaps you volunteered, or were asked, or possibly no one else came forward. Whatever your circumstances, the reality might not feel much like a vision! But that of itself doesn't mean you can't share in the school's vision, support its mission, or uphold its Christian ethos and values. Importantly, that doesn't mean you have to "buy into" anything you don't believe, or accept anything as an imposition. Your contribution as a governor is hugely important and, as with everything in life, it is all the more rewarding if you engage fully and actively with it. This means becoming a dynamic, active part of the vision and mission of the school.

Governors generally agree that they are appointed to ensure that their school is the very best it can possibly be – in other words, to uphold the vision and implement the mission. The challenge comes in how this is applied to the daily governance of the school, and how governors relate what they do, think and decide, to the bigger picture of why the school is there in the first place. In some small way every little thing that happens in a school – from the teaching methods to the toilets – is part and parcel of the vision. So an important part of your role is to hold everything up to scrutiny, championing anything that works towards the vision and challenging anything that blurs it.

The mission statement of the Church in Wales

A Church School is a witness to the mission of Christ in the Gospel:

- where Jesus Christ is our foundation;

- where every person has equal value and the chance to grow and develop to their full potential;

- where teachers, staff, governors and parents are committed to the education and development of the whole person;

- where the search for knowledge is accompanied by a quest for faith and a journey of spiritual experience;

so that…

- every child can learn of the richness of the created world, and grasp every opportunity to contribute to it in life;

- every member of staff can be nurtured in their vocation to teach;

- every achievement can be celebrated and every shortcoming forgiven;

- every person in this school can know that they are made in the image of God.

Every school should be a special place, a safe place, a place of learning, a place of nurture and of exploration. A school must demonstrate openness and acceptance, tolerance and forgiveness. Here, values and attitudes are formed and every individual is celebrated as unique.

A church school is all of these things and develops a distinctive Christian character through learning, religious education, prayer, worship and action in the name of Christ that makes God's love and presence known to the world.[5]

The Bishop of St Asaph, the Rt Revd Gregory Cameron, opening the nurture room in Gungrog C in W Nursery and Infant School. Photo by Simon Cameron.

Vision into mission

> The harvest is plentiful, but the labourers are
> few; therefore ask the Lord of the harvest to
> send out labourers into his harvest. Go on
> your way.
>
> ("The mission of the seventy", Luke 10:2-3)

It's great to have a big-picture vision, but not much good if we never put it into action. A school's mission should be the working-out of its vision – how it is implemented in order to bring it into reality. The mission of the Church in education is what governors have been called and appointed to. Once you come together as the people responsible for the governance of the school, you are part of a team in mission.

No one with any sense would set out on a highly demanding mission without first equipping themselves with as much information, knowledge and understanding as possible about what they are being asked to do – although sadly, many governors are asked to do just that. They do their best, but in order to stay true to the vision, governors themselves need training and formation. In some dioceses this is in short supply, owing to a serious lack of resources.

Equipping the governing body for the challenge

The following questions are offered for you to answer individually and then pool your responses. This will help to highlight both the strengths and areas for development concerning the whole governing body's understanding of the mission of the Church in education and, by extension, how it impacts your school.

Review	My response	Support required	Who can help?
What training have I received so far in the Church's mission in education?			
How often does our governing body discuss our core mission?			
How accessible & relevant do I find the DBE's documents?			
To what extent does our school mission statement accurately reflect what the school exists for?			
Does the mission statement need to be revisited by the whole community?			

All the forms and tables in this book can be downloaded from: www.rpdownloads.co.uk/Church-School-Governor-Resources_c_27.html, using the code: GOV001

Now pool your answers and agree what needs to be done, when and by whom. Keep this discussion as an ongoing item on your governors' agenda at meetings.

Taking up the mission

Seeing our children, young people and staff with the eyes of Christ is the challenge. When all is going well this appears pretty straightforward, but when the opposite is the case – when a young person is really struggling with disciplinary or mental health problems, when squabbles in the staff room or disagreements between governors arise, or when one of the staff isn't pulling their weight and it is affecting overall morale[6] – that is when it's all the more important to keep the vision and mission in mind.

A vision for the present and future

Just as a school exists to serve the local community it is situated in, so too it exists to serve the next generation as they go through the education system. Just as a teacher understands the importance of educating each generation for its time, so a governor has the task of translating the vision and mission of the Church and school into a new language – one that the children, young people, their families and the staff can understand and interpret for themselves.

Many governors have their own children in school, but even those who have daily contact with children and young people themselves come to realise that what applied when they were in school, or even ten years ago, will not necessarily be relevant now. The world is changing so fast that the issues of today are not the same as those of even the recent past. This sense of being out of kilter with the children and young people whom the governing body exists to serve can challenge a governor at a deeply personal level. As part of the leadership in a C of E or C in W school today, a governor needs to be familiar with the issues that young people are concerned with, and not too afraid if they are not their own issues. It is often in this area that many governors need particular guidance and support.

It can be very difficult, for example, to know how to respond to the case of a troubled young person. How can I help this pregnant teenager work towards a positive future for herself and her baby? What can I do for this lad who has been racially abused? What hope is there for the girl who is persistently in trouble with the police? In Chapter Four we will look at some specific challenges in more depth, but the message to take away from this is that upholding the vision at all times is paramount, especially when you're involved in the nitty-gritty of things.

Questioning minds

Young people have always been full of big questions. While we must be faithful to educating in the beliefs and values of Christianity in the Anglican tradition, so too it is essential, if young people are to develop a real aptitude for learning, that schools engage with the children's and young people's questions of purpose and meaning.

Much of what is taught is far broader now than it once was, incorporating areas of study that schools rarely if ever ventured into just a decade or so ago. The way in which ethical issues are included in the curriculum, for example, allows far greater room for personal exploration than it once did. In a good school these discussions and debates happen in all areas of learning, not just in religion, philosophy and ethics lessons. So in responding to the challenges of the time, governors need to be ready, willing and open to adapt to the reality of what is being taught, discussed and debated – while all the while keeping the vision undimmed before them.

Before we concern ourselves too much with what we are supposed to be doing as governors regarding teaching and the formation of children and young people, it is important that we listen to the questions that children and young people actually ask, rather than looking for answers to questions that they are not asking.

So let us begin with the questions that so many young people ask in school:

- Who am I really?

- Why was I born?

- What's the point of my life?

Equally interesting for many is the big question asked by Jesus himself:

- Who do you say that I am? (Mark 8:29)

Without realising it, these questioning young people, who appear in every class, are asking the key questions about why the Church is so committed to its mission in education.

So often our children and young people do not believe they are special, unique or worthy. Psychologists tell us that the human mind deals with up to 50,000 thoughts each day, of which 70 per cent are negative! The world of advertising has become so skilled in getting exposure to the human mind that it now works on the fact that it picks up at least 16,000 messages a day. And what are these messages? "You need this product, or that gadget, because you are clearly deficient without it." Sadly, it works. Our mission is to teach the children to discern what is real and of value – to show another way that brings lasting joy and fulfilment in communities of learning and formation. Our schools must be places where young people develop a passion for truth and justice, as stewards committed to equality and respect for all. Our challenge is to continue to make this world fit for our children.

Reflection

- How do you feel personally about what you have taken on?

- How does the vision of the school chime with your own personal vision?

- How do you feel about undertaking a "mission" and how can you turn the school's vision into a mission – both as an individual and with your fellow governors?

A vision of God

Above and beyond all the vision and mission statements and talk of ethos and values there exists something intangible that defies description. To Christians, this is the mystery of God. St Paul put it most eloquently when he wrote to the Corinthians:

> For now we see in a mirror, dimly, but then we will see face to face. Now I know only in part; then I will know fully, even as I have been fully known.
>
> (1 Corinthians 13:12)

What St Paul is articulating here is not God, but the human limitation and yearning to see God "face to face". Christians come close to it in following the example of Jesus Christ in everything they say, think and do. Even for those who are not practising Christians, the example of Christ can – and indeed should – be a guiding inspiration when we are thinking about the ethos and values of a Christian school.

So how can this work in real life? Well, in Chapter One we saw how a church school should strive for real inclusivity – welcoming and valuing children and young people from all backgrounds, faith groups and walks of life and respecting all members of staff, governors and parents as equals. In the three years of his ministry, Christ was nothing if not inclusive. Indeed, he frequently exasperated and enraged the elitist and discriminatory authorities by consorting with people who, for one reason or another, were despised, cast out, considered inferior or not to be touched.

Among Jesus' friends and followers were tax collectors, despised by the rest of society (Luke 19:1-10), disgraced women (Luke 7:36-50), disabled people (Mark 10:46-52) and those who were sick (Mark 1:40-45). The parable of the Good Samaritan (Luke 10:25-37) was radical and provocative, because in it Jesus recognised and valued the humanity of a foreigner, who would normally have been considered alien and shunned.

The examples above are just a few of many instances of Jesus' radical inclusivity and uncompromising compassion. In Jewish society, people who were ritually "unclean" in some way were perceived as damaging to the relationship with God – not only for themselves, but also for their community and by extension wider society. In including those who were considered unclean, Christ was turning around people's concepts of who could relate to God and how. It must have taken real courage to teach these things – a lone voice speaking out for justice in a culture where prejudice and exclusion were considered not only necessary, but virtuous. It culminated in Peter's vision in Acts (10:9-16), which made it clear that everyone could and should have a relationship with God. So while Christ was including and humanising people who were suffering, he was also making it possible for them to get their relationship with God right.

As we have seen, Christianity has inclusiveness at its foundation, based on the ability of all to relate to God, which is why the Church has a vocation to be there for everyone in the community, no matter who, and why all governors from all walks of life and faith backgrounds or none, should share the vision of inclusivity and compassion.

All who saw it began to grumble and said, "He has gone to be the guest of one who is a sinner." Zacchaeus stood there and said to the Lord, "Look, half of my possessions, Lord, I will give to the poor; and if I have defrauded anyone of anything, I will pay back four times as much." Then Jesus said to him, "Today salvation has come to this house… For the Son of Man came to seek out and to save the lost."

(Luke 19:7-10)

Therefore, I tell you, her sins, which were many, have been forgiven; hence she has shown great love.

(Luke 7:47)

Reflection

Take a little time out and find a quiet space to reflect on the Bible verses you have read in this section. Then ask yourself:

- What do they mean to you and how might they apply to your life and your work as a governor? Are there any stumbling blocks?

- Do you have a personal vision for your life? Is it consistent with your work as a governor? Does it chime with the vision of the school? If not, why not?

ENDNOTES

1 The National Society: www.christianvalues4schools.co.uk
2 Neville Norcross, *Christian Values for Church Schools: Making Them Count* (Cambridge: Grove Books, 2014).
3 Tim Elbourne, *Understanding Church Schools: Ideas for Today from Joshua Watson's Founding Vision* (Cambridge: Grove Books, 2012).
4 Statutory Inspection of Anglican and Methodist Schools. For more about this, see Chapter Six.
5 The Church in Wales/Life/Schools/Mission: www.churchinwales.org.uk
6 Chapter Four looks in more depth at some of the particular challenges you may face as a governor.

CHAPTER 3

A CRITICAL FRIEND:
The role of the individual governor

In Chapter Two we looked at how important it is for governors to keep the vision of the Church and the school uppermost in their minds in every action they carry out and every decision they take. What's also true however is that governors are busy people whose time is often at a premium. The barrage of documents and emails that land in the in-tray and in-box can feel quite overwhelming, particularly if the school is due an inspection. (You can read more about how to prepare for that in Chapter Six.) In addition, a governor can feel personally out of his or her depth with some of the challenging situations that arise, and at a loss as to the best way forward.

The real challenge of governorship comes into play when, faced with so many demands on their time and expertise, governors are tempted simply to address what appears to be the most pressing matter, or to go along with the consensus despite perhaps having personal reservations. No matter how important or urgent something seems, and no matter that you have a niggling doubt about something that everyone else seems to agree about – it still needs to be held up to scrutiny as to whether it is true to the big picture – in other words, the vision and mission.

In order to create and especially to retain governors who are willing and able to rise to this challenge, it is essential that each new governor in a church school has an excellent induction – a solid grounding in the day-to-day running of the school, as well as a clear understanding of its over-arching vision and mission. To keep this in focus, it's vitally important that every governor has a continuous and robust process of review and self-evaluation in place, to identify his or her strengths and weaknesses and raise his or her knowledge and confidence to be able to say:

- I understand the mission of the Church in education.

- I am clear about how the school I serve seeks to fulfil that.

- I know why I am here and I understand my role.

- I know what steps I need to take to develop in my role.

- I feel confident in asking questions and seeking clarification.

- I know how to raise concerns and where to go for help.

A critical friend

It is probably fair to say that the role of the governor has undergone many changes over the past twenty years, particularly where government expectations are concerned. A variety of government papers and guidelines[1] have articulated three key aspects of the role of governor. In essence, there are three core responsibilities:

- Playing a strategic role.

- Being a critical friend.

- Ensuring accountability.[2]

What is a critical friend?

John Cox, Director of Education in the Diocese of St Edmundsbury and Ipswich (1995-2006) defines a "critical friend" as someone who:

- Recognises and celebrates the achievements and strengths of the school.

- Knows where there are weaknesses and where the school is not performing as well as it should be.

- Gives support and encouragement in bringing about improvements.

- Is fully involved in plans for developments and improvements.

- Maintains the balance between support and change.[3]

Governor induction

The effectiveness of the whole governing body is dependent on the ability of each member to contribute to the best of their ability. For a new governor the first few meetings can be very daunting, and it is important that she or he feels welcomed and valued.

The induction of new governors varies greatly, but a good induction is essential if a governor is going to be able to contribute fully to discussions and decisions. Every governing body should have someone responsible for governor induction.

The *Ofsted Governors' Handbook*[4] is an important guide for all governors. However, it is generic and, although helpful, can't help with all the particular characteristics of your school. In the following section we will look at how one school has addressed these issues.

The Governor Induction Pack – a case study

"The origin of the Governor Induction Pack dates back to the time when I was elected as a parent governor at a state school where, despite being enthusiastic and well intentioned, I found myself floundering, confused and over-awed by the level of responsibility I was taking on and the role I was expected to play.

"As a newcomer, I naively expected to be helped, if not spoon-fed, with a ready selection of 'how to' guides, but I soon realised that this was not the case. My colleagues on the governing body pointed me towards publicly available information, although I personally found the usual prescribed sources of help somewhat detached from my experience as a new governor.

"When I was asked to join the governing body as a foundation governor, I was again over-awed – this time for a different reason. I was humbled to be asked to join what was an already outstanding body of governors. Having finally accepted, it was my resolve to continue developing myself – but more importantly to ensure that any new governor we recruited would not have to endure the lengthy apprenticeship that I had served. It furthered my conviction that from the outset governors should be clear about their purpose and equipped with the knowledge and skills to ensure clear, strategic direction and to promote the ethos and values of our community, in order ultimately to deliver the high standards and outcomes for our children. In short, new governors should be able to join the body and 'hit the ground running'. It was my intention to demystify the role of governor without trivialising it, and to provide an at-a-glance guide without skirting round issues. The Induction Pack was devised.

"By devising our own bespoke guide based around the characteristics of our school, a dual purpose was served; not only were governors able to learn the ropes quickly, but it also helped to promote and safeguard our distinctive and essential Christian character. It does not claim, however, to have transformative properties, to be the fount of all knowledge, nor does it hold all the answers – it continues to be a work in progress. But when it is used – and this is the key – in conjunction with a mentor, this in theory should enable the words to be brought to life in a meaningful way, as the mentor metaphorically handholds the new recruit through the induction process.

"It is an exercise in commitment and faith towards a common goal, providing our children with the education they deserve, and fulfilling the Church's mission to form and educate our young people to be builders of a society fit for the next generation."

"The Induction Pack was very comprehensive in terms of factual content, and not only did it give me a clear idea of what was expected, but the governor in charge of induction was able to take me through it and bring to life some of the more specific advice, making it meaningful in the context of the school's governing body, and in particular our Anglican ethos". (Parent governor)

Governors of C in W or C of E schools are so much more than a set of skills or competencies. Being a governor takes a lot more than having a passing interest or commitment alone. The simple purpose of a customised Induction Pack is to enable each governor to get on with the job, adding their unique contribution to the greater whole.

Over time the school in the illustration on the previous page has responded to the changing needs of governors and developed a comprehensive programme. Your Diocesan Board of Education (DBE) should be able to provide guidance as to which schools have a good induction process. Here is a contents list, designed to help you get started on compiling your own:

Induction Pack contents

- The governors' schedule/terms of reference.

- The school mission statement.

- Governors' prayer (see Chapter Seven for suggestions).

- A copy of the school prospectus.

- The roles and responsibilities of school governors.

- Instrument of Government (applies to Voluntary Aided schools only).

- A copy of the trust deed of the DBE.

- A copy of the foundation governors' handbook, if appropriate.

- The Governing Body Code of Practice (which should be available from the DBE).

- A list of governors' statutory responsibilities.

- Information about inspection procedures and guidelines.

- A model policy for governors when visiting school. (Each school will have its protocols surrounding governors visiting. These should be outlined in the Induction Pack.)

- Visit report template. (A blueprint for producing a report after your visit.)

- Mentor contact details.

- Further resources, relevant journals, etc.

Know the school

Whether you are a first-time governor or have been doing it for years, it is important to keep refreshing and updating what you know about the school, and to get to know it at a deeper level. So often, our perception of something is a bigger factor in influencing our judgements than the truth, so the governing body needs an accurate picture of what is actually happening in the school, as opposed to what they might think is the case. A school that has long enjoyed an excellent reputation can so easily slip into "coasting" mode, rather than looking creatively for the next steps and continually striving for excellence. A governor needs to stay alert to that, and getting to know the school is one of the best ways to go about it.

Feeling part of the school community is not easy if you are not at least familiar with the premises and, most important of all, the people. One Chair of Governors has created a simple checklist to see how well governors know their staff and the premises.

Having received the results of the survey, the Chair of Governors explores ways of helping each governor become better acquainted with the school community.

Some creative ways of getting to know the school

Governor open days

Governors are invited to sign up to observe the activities that the children and young people are engaged with throughout the day.

Advice: Try to get a range of experiences both in the classroom and outside it. Remember it is the children's and young people's experience that you are really trying to find out about.

How well do you know the school?	Comments
Have you met all the staff?	
Do you know your way around the school site?	
Are you familiar with the school day & class structure?	
Any other comments:	
Please return this form to the Chair of Governors	

Back to school

Here each governor is allocated a "buddy" and joins the class for the day to experience it. Without exception, he or she does everything that the children and young people do. This is a great way of gaining a pupil's perspective.

Advice: Select a year group that you know the least about, so that you can gain as much as possible from the experience. Ask as many questions as you need to, and be sure to live their day with them – do as they do.

Work experience

In this activity the governor is adopted for the day by a member of the support staff and again sees the day from their perspective – doing as much with the member of staff as is possible and appropriate.

Advice: Arrive and depart at the same time. Choose an area that you know little about, so that you really see the extent of the responsibilities and challenges that the staff face, as well as areas in which they really excel.

Headteacher for a day

This can be one of the most eye-opening fact-finding experiences. Without altering anything of the head's day, join the head from the moment of arrival until he or she departs in the evening.

Advice: Get a good night's sleep before you undertake this activity – it may be a very long day!

An invitation to tea

A small group of governors invite a cross-section of children and young people from one Key Stage to afternoon tea in school. Make it really special – cups and saucers, sandwiches and cakes. During tea, ask the children to talk about their school. What they enjoy, really like – and what they would like to change.

Advice: Six to eight pupils is enough. Choose a special setting so that this really is an occasion. Invite pupils from the same Key Stage, to keep the discussion on equal terms. Keep your questions open-ended, so that the children and young people are able to respond as fully as possible in their own way.

Evaluating the individual governor

No one has all the answers or skills – which is why governors are drawn from a diverse variety of backgrounds. One complements the other. However, it is good to carry out a skills audit of each member of the governing body, to see where each governor's real strengths lie. This helps in the formulation of the committees and also with working out whom to allocate for the oversight of the different areas of the school.

The following is a model skills audit given to individual governors by the Chair of one school, with the aim of inviting governors to take on responsibilities that make best use of their skills and experience. You will notice that the end column is headed "Interest". This enabled the Chair and the governor responsible for professional development to see where members might benefit from training, enabling them to move into the area/s they were interested in.

Individual governor skills audit			
Name:			
Date:			
How would you rate your knowledge, experience & interest on a scale of 1-5, where 1 = little or none, and 5 = extensive?			
Areas of expertise	**Knowledge**	**Experience**	**Interest**
Strategic planning			
Vision & mission of this school			
Marketing			
Project management			
Presentation			
Research			
Training			
Team-working			
Legal knowledge			
Chairing meetings			
Clerking meetings			
Administration			
Awareness of information/sources			
School improvement plan (SIP)			
Self-evaluation Form (SEF)[5]			
School profile			
Strengths & weaknesses of the school			
Short- & long-term school priorities			
The Ofsted inspection process relating to Sections 48 & 5, or the Estyn inspection process relating to Sections 50 & 5[6]			
Curriculum			
Spiritual, moral, social & cultural (SMSC) education			
Religious education			
Early Years/Foundation			
Infants (Key Stage 1)			
Juniors (Key Stage 2)			

Areas of expertise	Knowledge	Experience	Interest
Maths/numeracy			
English/literacy			
Science			
PE/sport			
Art/design/creative curriculum			
Information communications technology (ICT)			
Personal, social, health & economic (PSHE)			
Languages (please state which)			
Extracurricular activities			
Extended schools services (such as hiring out school premises or sports facilities to an external body)			
Special educational needs (SEN)			
Premises			
School building & maintenance			
Health & safety			
Contracting services			
Premises management			
People			
Well-being (staff)			
Public relations			
Communication			
Listening			
Mediating			
Personnel management			
Recruiting/interviewing			
Equal opportunities			
Performance management			
Continuing professional development (CPD)			

Areas of expertise	Knowledge	Experience	Interest
Finance			
Financial planning			
School financial management			
Best value			
Relevant experience			
Please give further details of any work-related/personal experience you can bring to this governing body.			
Training			
Have you undertaken the governor induction course? (please circle)	Yes/No		
If yes, was it arranged by the diocese or local education authority?			
Please give brief details of courses you have undertaken in the past three years – include governor training and/or work-based training	Diocese/LEA		
Other training			
Would you like more information on a particular topic, or is there a particular subject you would like training in?			

ENDNOTES

1. Such as: *Guidance on Good Governance* (DfEE, 1996); *Roles of Governing Bodies and Head Teachers* (2000).
2. www.gov.uk/government/publications/governance-handbook
3. John Cox, *Critical Friend* (Stowmarket: Kevin Mayhew, 2013).
4. Department for Education, *Governors' Handbook for Governors in Maintained Schools, Academies and Free Schools* (January 2014).
5. This is an official form, which relates to the inspections detailed in Sections 48/50 & 5 of the Education Act 2005.
6. For more about this turn to Chapter Six.

CHAPTER 4

WHEN THE GOING GETS TOUGH: Some of the challenges facing governors of church schools

Although the role of governor can be one of the most rewarding things you can do, it can of course also be one of the most challenging. Challenges – as you may well have experienced for yourself – can crop up in any number of ways. Among the most common are:

- Disagreements and differences – with fellow governors, the headteacher, or external bodies such as the local authority or Diocesan Board of Education (DBE).

- Times when it may be difficult to uphold the school's Christian values and ethos, or to reconcile conflicting viewpoints.

- Problems recruiting and retaining staff.

- Discipline – with children and young people, staff and parents.

- The spectre of "radicalisation" – whether real or imagined – which hangs over many schools in the current climate.

- Difficult relationships with the local church and parish community.

Disagreements

The Bible is full of disagreements and disputes – from the sibling rivalry between Jacob and Esau in Genesis (25:22-34), to bitter divisions among the people of the early Christian Church in Corinth (1 Corinthians 1:10-17). From a distance, their squabbles exasperated St Paul, who in his letters entreated them to drop their differences and keep their eye on the vision.

> I appeal to you, brothers and sisters, by the name of our Lord Jesus Christ, that all of you should by in agreement and that there should be no divisions among you, but that you should be united in the same mind and the same purpose.
>
> (1 Corinthians 1:10)

Not much has changed over the millennia, and it's probably fair to say that every community experiences its share of spats, squabbles and storms. That doesn't necessarily mean that anyone is doing a bad job, or that the system is broken – but it does mean that something needs to be addressed. One of the hardest things a governor can do is stand up for what is right, or challenge something that seems wrong, especially if doing so might run the risk of ruffling feathers, rocking the boat, or even unleashing a storm. But as we saw in Chapter Three, that's just what a critical friend is called upon to do when necessary.

When a disagreement or difference appears irreconcilable, particularly if it threatens to disrupt the smooth running of the school, there should be help and mediation support available from several sources. Here are some questions that may provide some pointers in dealing with it:

- Is there a formal process for managing it?

- Is there any guidance from the DBE?

- Is it worth bringing to the attention of an independent adjudicator (perhaps the Chair of Governors from a nearby school)?

- If it has become personal or bitter, would some pastoral counselling help all parties to move on?

Above all, what is important is that everything is done in a spirit of honesty, generosity and compassion. For Christians, Christ is the supreme example of this. In addition, the Christian service of Holy Communion (also known as the Eucharist) provides us with a model for reconciliation. The Eucharistic president greets us with "The Lord be with you," and we answer, "And also with you." Then, according to local custom, we may greet each other with a handshake, saying, "Peace be with you." This may take place before Holy Communion. Symbolically, it is important that people are "right" with one another before they presume to draw near to God.

Reflection

- Can you think of a time when you stood up for what was right, even though it might have been unpopular?

- Can you think of a time when someone challenged you, or said something you were unwilling to hear? How did you react?

- In both cases, how might you do things differently now?

- Is there anything in your school that you ought to challenge?

- Can you relate to the idea of sharing the peace in order to be "right" with other people, before approaching God?

Put away from you all bitterness and wrath and anger and wrangling and slander, together with all malice, and be kind to one another, tender-hearted, forgiving one another, as God in Christ has forgiven you.

(Ephesians 4:31-32)

Upholding the school's Christian values and ethos

As we saw in Chapter Two, having a clear vision and a well understood set of values is essential to all Church in Wales (C in W) or Church of England (C of E) schools. The challenge for governors is not only to uphold these values in their own work, but also to ensure that they are embedded in and practised throughout the whole school community. This applies equally to day-to-day school life and to wider policies.

As we shall see in the following sections, there are two areas in particular where governors may feel conflicted – namely, admissions and collective worship. Of course a great deal depends on the circumstances and nature of your particular school, but whatever that is, it's important to give it time for discussion, reflection and prayer – both individually and as a group.

Admissions

It's a bit of a running joke that parents who want their child to go to a church school suddenly become pious and start to attend church. It's also the case that for some of these parents it is a route to rediscovered faith. Whether or not governors should be concerned about "pew jumping", or implement policies to try to curb the practice, is a moot point. But it is testament to church schools' high record of achievement (more about that in Chapter One) and their reputation as places where children and young people will receive a good all-round education – academically, socially and culturally. There is a more

serious side to it, of course, and in recent years church schools' admissions policies have become an increasingly important, and sometimes controversial, issue that governors have to contend with.

Governors in Voluntary Aided (VA) schools, academies and free schools have a duty as the admissions authority to determine and enforce admissions policy. In Voluntary Controlled (VC) schools, admissions are determined by the local authority (for more about the various types of school, turn to Chapter One). For any school of any type there are a number of statutory provisions determining particular groups (such as children in public care, or looked after children[1]) who take priority. The clerk to the governing body and the DBE should be able to advise on these. It is also important to recognise that government admissions policies can change over time, and this will have an impact on new admissions and the general make-up of the pupil population.

Before specifics are defined in an admissions policy, governors need to consider what they are trying to achieve. In preparation for an agenda item on this, try answering the following questions:

As a governing body, through our admissions policy, how can we explicitly state and provide evidence that we have achieved the following?

- Compliance with our statutory obligations.

- An intentional response to the Gospel imperative to love our neighbour as ourselves (Mark 12:31).

- Upholding and advancing the Christian nature and character of the school.

- Compliance with DBE requirements and guidance.

- Meeting the needs of the local neighbourhood (in particular its ethnic and socio-economic profile).

- Admitting a pupil cohort that, both as a year group and as the whole school community, reflects our inclusive values (and supports our mission statement) and is workable for the teaching and support community.

In recent years there have been both local initiatives and national guidance on the most appropriate way in which to apply admissions policies in all schools, especially in over-subscribed C of E and C in W schools. In 2011 the National Society issued an advisory document[2] in order to "provide Diocesan Boards of Education and governors' Admissions Committees with some over-arching considerations."[3]

In particular the National Society/Board of Education undertook a survey to gain an insight into the balance between places offered to church families and to the local community. On the whole it was found that there was no conflict between these two groups and that the intake for primary schools in particular represented the local neighbourhood. However, for some particularly over-subscribed schools this may not be the case. It is then up to the governors to decide what criteria to apply.

Questions for discussion may include but not be restricted to:

- Religious affiliation.

- How that should be defined:

    ◦ Attendance at worship.

    ◦ Attendance at other church-related activities.

    ◦ Religious affiliation to a particular denomination. (For example, should a Methodist family who frequently attend church take priority over a less frequently attending Anglican family?)

    ◦ Religious affiliation to another faith (Should a devout family of a faith other than Christanity take priority over an Anglican or other Christian family who, for example, may attend Church infrequently or not at all? Often families of other faiths choose to send their children to C of E or C in W schools, because they are places where faith will be respected and taken seriously.[4]

    ◦ The time period over which that behaviour is measured.

- Should siblings of current pupils take priority (even though the younger sibling may not qualify for admission under the criteria for that cohort)?

- Should the criteria be applied to one or both parents or the child?

A balance needs to be found in any church school admissions policy between ensuring that the school has a distinctive Christian ethos, meeting the needs of the local community and witnessing to the wider Gospel imperative and message of inclusivity.

In 2013 an interview with Justin Welby the Archbishop of Canterbury attracted a considerable amount of media attention, due to the apparently contradictory statements he made regarding the extent to which faith-based criteria should inform admissions policies. It appears that Welby's point was that church schools were playing a key part in tackling community cohesion, especially in poor areas and that the overriding criterion should be local need. Governors, as members of the local community, and perhaps even more so than local authority governors, are best placed to observe, interpret and apply what is needed in their local community.

The Church of England Chief Education Officer and General Secretary of the National Society, the Revd Nigel Genders, gave an interview in 2014 about the new need to expand school places nationally.[5] He said that he expected an open approach to be taken to school admissions, and that new C of E schools would be "rooted in Christian heritage", without necessarily having Christian pupils.

Above all, governors should ensure that whatever criteria they use are clearly defined and transparent. Again, the DBE can help in this. The National Society report concludes by stating that "schools should be able to show how their Admissions policy and practice demonstrates the school's commitment both to distinctiveness and inclusivity, to church families and the wider community."[6]

Collective worship

A significant challenge for governors and staff in C of E and C in W schools is collective worship. The School Standards and Framework Act 1998 states that:

> each pupil in attendance at a community, foundation or voluntary school shall on each school day take part in an act of collective worship. [7]

In an environment where many or most of the pupils may or may not be accustomed to collective worship in whatever faith tradition, or may or may not be Christian, how is this to be achieved? It is an area where there are constant challenges by government, by think tanks, by activist groups. These are usually along the lines of:

- The increasingly multicultural nature of society in the UK.

- How worship according to a particular tradition of belief system leads to division rather than community cohesion.

This is a key area where governors need to take a lead and support the headteacher and staff. The next section considers some of the steps governors can take to help:

Getting to know the school, the pupils, the parents, the local community and the staff

What is right for one particular school or even class may not be right for another. For example, in a C in W or C of E school in a predominately white Christian area, a "traditional" assembly with readings, prayers and hymns may be appropriate. In a more diverse area, sharing and celebrating the key aspects of Abrahamic faiths (Christianity, Judaim and Islam) might be a better approach. Children, especially of primary (KS1 and KS2) age, are naturally curious about why they are different from one another. Practical demonstrations of how various feasts can be celebrated at home and in places of worship (the church, the mosque, the synagogue) are another way in which teaching can be made real and reinforced. Christianity has become weak in integrating the private and public expression of rites of passage and the rituals associated with them and a lot can be learnt from other faiths in this respect.

Governors' skills

Many governors of C of E or C in W schools will be members of their local parish churches. This can include those who actively participate in leading worship – as preachers, lectors, intercessors and those who have a liturgical role. These people are well-equipped with both skills and experience to lead public worship in schools. Governors may be children's work leaders (Sunday School, Junior Church, Messy Church, Godly Play) who are used to relating and presenting a clear and engaging message to children. Other skills (public speaking, drama, even puppetry or magic) could be useful too.

Staff skills

Leading assemblies and acts of worship shouldn't necessarily be the preserve of the headteacher. It may well be that other members of staff have skills or experience in this area which make them better able to take a leadership role. As a governor, a critical friend, it may be necessary to point out to a headteacher that others are better placed to perform this function.

Encouraging the appointment of a lead governor for collective worship

If there isn't one already, a governor who has skills and expertise in this area, in whom the head has confidence, and who has the time and flexibility to attend many if not all of the acts of worship in the school, could be an invaluable resource.

Skills of local clergy and church leaders

Further on in this chapter we will look at relationships with the local church, in particular local clergy and others in leadership positions. In the meantime, again being an active and involved critical friend can prove invaluable in identifying who among local clergy and church leadership may be effective in leading assemblies and who might be encouraged into another role.

Children's and young people's skills

How can children and young people be enabled and empowered to lead worship? As a governor, especially one with a pupil liaison role, it could be appropriate to support and enable them to take a peer leadership role in providing collective worship.

Establishing relationships with leaders of other faiths

Good relationships with leaders of other faith groups are crucial especially in areas and schools where non-Christian faiths predominate. Having the

Questions for discussion at governor meetings:

- What do we want to achieve by our daily act of worship?

- What are the constraints on this:

    ◦ Space for the whole school to meet?

    ◦ Time?

- Effective worship leadership – what do we mean by that?

- Skills of a good worship leader in our community:

    ◦ What are they?

    ◦ Who has them?

    ◦ How can we train and empower new worship leaders?

occasional assembly led by non-Christian leaders can help good community relationships and enable children and young people to relate their personal faith to other belief systems in a wider context.

Recruitment and retention of staff

Governing bodies have considerable responsibilities for the staff they employ.[8] In general terms, governors rely on the staff to:

- Deliver the overall management plan and policies that the governors have agreed.

- Develop, sustain and reflect the Christian ethos of the school.

- Provide the best possible education for the pupils in their care.

- Maintain a safe and stimulating working environment for pupils and colleagues.

In their turn, governors need to ensure that staff have the resources and institutional framework to enable this to happen, and that this takes place in a context of a clear understanding of Christian leadership. The exact nature of the relationship depends on the legal status of the school. In VC schools, teaching staff are employees of the local authority, whereas in VA schools and academies, teaching staff are employees of the governing body (for more about this turn to Chapter One). The appointment of headteachers is governed at a national level, with a partnership between the local authority, the DBE and the governing body.[9] In the recruitment process governors of VA schools may then discriminate in favour of candidates who demonstrate a positive commitment to the Christian faith and its expression in the school. However, governors need to be clear about what they mean by this. What is meant by "Anglican practising communicant"? What is meant by "practising Christian"? The level of seniority of the position may also be a consideration. For example, while it may not necessarily be essential for a teaching assistant to be a practising Christian, different criteria will apply for senior leadership posts, such as a year head. Again the DBE will have standard guidelines for wording of job descriptions and advertisements.

In each appointment it is important to find a balance between the candidate's professional capabilities, skills and experience, their religious affiliation and faith and the needs of the school.

Discipline

Discipline is another responsibility for governing bodies. This may be one of the most challenging aspects of the role, as it involves difficult and potentially life-changing decisions for those involved. There are many statutory procedures which need to be followed which apply in all schools. In addition, for governors in C of E and C in W schools, procedures should be followed in the light of the Christian ethos and values of the school and in the context of Christian charity. This does not mean a soft or lenient approach, but rather following the example of Christ (for example, John 8:1-11) and taking into account the needs both of the individual concerned and the wider community.

Radicalisation in schools

In recent years there have been many reports and rumours of some staff in schools using their privileged position of trust inappropriately and attempting to indoctrinate and radicalise pupils and other staff. The popular media may be perpetuating the myth that all faith-based schools are there to brainwash children and young people, but thankfully this is extremely uncommon in C of E and C in W schools. Governors can help to avoid this association by making sure the school builds and maintains good relationships with the local communities they serve, and being clear and transparent about their aims and objectives.

Relationships with local church and wider communities

All partnerships need work, and this is as true for C of E and C in W schools and the local church and parish. Churches may see schools as a way to reach local families who might not otherwise have any relationship with the church, or who are using it simply to gain admission. The schools themselves may see their status as a way of achieving an over-subscribed and high-quality application cohort which in turn enhances results. Neither should be the case. Schools should welcome the opportunity to be involved in the life of the wider Church in their locality, with all the advantages that can bring for teaching and learning. In turn, churches need to welcome and embrace the opportunity to be involved in the nurture of the young and to go back to Joshua Watson's vision of using church schools for the advancement of individuals and society.

Reflection

- As a governing body, find three words which describe your current relationship with your local parish church and clergy.

- As a governing body, find three ideas you can offer your local parish church and clergy.

- What support would you like to receive from your local parish church and clergy?

ENDNOTES

[1] Department for Education *et al.*: www.gov.uk

[2] The Archbishops' Council & the National Society, *Admissions to Church of England Schools* (June 2011): www.churchofengland.org/media/1513919/nsadmissionsguidancejune2011final%20(3).pdf

[3] Ibid., paragraph 3.

[4] Ibid., paragraph 11.

[5] Adam Lusher, "New Church of England schools to adopt 'open admissions' policy", in *The Independent* (11 June 2014).

[6] The Archbishops' Council & the National Society, Admissions to Church of England Schools (June 2011).

[7] School Standards and Framework Act 1998, Section 70: www.legislation.gov.uk/ukpga/1998/31/pdfs/ukpga_19980031_en.pdf

[8] The Archbishops' Council & the National Society, *Selecting, Appointing and Developing Staff in Church Schools* (2001, 2009): www.churchofengland.org/media/1386673/selecting%20appointing%20developing%20staff%20in%20ce%20schools%202009.pdf

[9] School Standards and Framework Act, 1988.

CHAPTER 5

ON MESSAGE – ON MISSION – ON TASK:
Induction, review and self-evaluation for the governing body

There is no lack of material from local authorities and support agencies offering help and advice to governors as to how to go about a review and self-evaluation of governance. Therefore it is not the intention to reinvent the wheel in this chapter. What is important is to consider is how a governing body and the individual governors of a Church in Wales (C in W) or Church of England (C of E) school might go about the process.

In Chapter Six we will look at how to prepare specifically for a school inspection, and specially tailored resources are offered to help with that. We will also see how critical it is that review and self-evaluation don't just take place in a flurry of activity leading up to an inspection, but are perceived by governors, the headteacher and staff as a continuous and ongoing process.

Review and self-evaluation should establish what difference governors make in the effective running and delivery of education in the school. Governors ought to be able to provide clear evidence of the impact of their governance, although this is a particular area where some need help.

> During the diocesan inspection of schools carried out under Ofsted Section 48, I have often come across headteachers who tell me theirs is a very supportive and effective governing body. However, when asked the question, "Can you tell me about the impact you feel your governing body has on the leadership of this school?" they sometimes find it very difficult to answer. It often takes quite a bit of digging to discover the true worth of their governance.
>
> Sr Judith Russi, Director, Educarem

Where and how to start
A good place to start is with a reflective training session that looks at the whole governing body's understanding of their school's mission.

Review & self-evaluation – our effectiveness in the mission of the Church in education today	
As a governing body, reflect together on each of the following questions:	
How informed are you as a governor about the mission of the Church in education?	
What is the mission for your school today? (answer this without reference to any mission statement that already exists)	
Do all governors agree on your priorities for mission?	
Do you think the mission statement is known & understood by the governors?	
... by the teachers?	
... by the children & young people?	
... by the parents?	
Is the mission statement accessible to everyone listed above?	
What evidence is there to show the impact of the mission statement on all aspects of school life?	
How often is the mission statement reviewed?	

Every aspect of life within the school must be consistent with the core purpose, mission statement, aims and objectives of the school as a Christian learning community. You may find the following table helpful in checking how well equipped you and your governing body are for that.

Review & self-evaluation – the next steps	
To what extent are we educating young people to challenge, change & transform the society in which they live? **What evidence is there to support our views?**	
To what extent are we fulfilling the needs of those in the greatest need? **What evidence is there to support our views?**	
To what extent is our school a place of hope, built on our belief that everyone carries a unique gift? **What evidence is there to support our views?**	
To what extent have we considered & begun to include in our strategic planning areas of development that address the above? **What evidence is there to support this?**	

Review & self-evaluation – continued	
To what extent are we engaging with the parish & local community, to be a place of welcome for all? **What evidence is there to support this?**	
As a governing body, what are our next steps?	

A framework for systematic review and self-evaluation

Although each diocese may vary in its approach to the Section 48 (SIAMS) or Section 50 (Gwella) inspections (for more on these, turn to Chapter Six), the following broad areas will be evaluated:

Leadership and management at all levels

Governors

- Does the governing body have a clear mission and purpose?

- What is the impact of its governance on all key areas of the life of the school?

- To what extent do governors witness to a Christ-centred learning community?

Headteacher

- Is he or she striving for excellence?

- Is he or she innovative and inspirational, and both strong and compassionate as a leader?

- To what extent does he or she demonstrate clear vision, based on the teachings of the Gospel and the Church?

Senior and middle leaders

- Are they confident in carrying out the mission of the Church in education, striving for excellence?

- Are they empowered risk-takers who know how to translate the vision and mission of the school into their areas of responsibility?

- Do their policies and priorities take into account those in the greatest need?

Student leadership

- Are the children and young people striving to be the best they can be?

- Are they inspired and confident in taking on leadership roles which may be counter-cultural?

- Are they religiously literate and able to articulate the purpose and meaning of their learning as part of their development as people of challenge, change and transformation?

Overall effectiveness

- Across the board, how effective is the school in fulfilling its mission, aims and objectives?

- What is the impact of the school on the children and young people, and on the local and wider community?

- Is the school a beacon of hope for all?

The school as a Christian community

The school community

- Does everyone (children and young people, staff and families) feel valued and respected?

- How is this experienced at each level?

The community

- How does the school impact on the local community and engage with the wider community, nationally and globally?

Curriculum religious education

Attainment, achievement and progress in RE

- Is RE a leading area of attainment and achievement?

Quality of teaching

- Are the children and young people receiving the best possible religious education, which is relevant, challenging and engaging with the big questions of the twenty-first century?

- Are they religiously literate?

- Are they encouraged to think deeply about spiritual matters, to appreciate difference and tolerance, and to make links between what they are learning and the world about them?

Leadership and management of RE

- Is RE a leading example of excellence in the school?

- Are the staff empowered and encouraged to be innovative, creative and take on responsibility for their own learning and faith development?

Children's and young people's spiritual, moral, social and cultural education and development

- Are there clear links and connections made in all areas of learning and exploration, which ask the big questions of purpose and meaning, drawing on Anglican beliefs and values?

- Is this led as a key area – well planned, delivered, monitored and assessed?

Evaluating the school's spiritual, moral, social and cultural education

Spiritual, moral, social and cultural education (SMSC) is the first entitlement of each child and young person in the country. Regardless of faith background, every school must educate spiritually, morally, socially and culturally. (Turn to Chapter Six to find out more about the critical importance of SMSC when it comes to school inspections.) Look at the following table and discuss your understanding of each of these areas. This is not easy for schools that do not have a faith foundation, as it is difficult to find a common core set of beliefs and values that inform policy and procedure.

Defining & evaluating SMSC education		
Title area	**Definition**	**Evidence – where & what to look for**
Spiritual	Christian values & beliefs about the meaning & purpose of life – who we are, why we are here & where we are going. *Key points*: • We are created in love & for love. • All human beings are equally & unconditionally God's children. • Each one is entrusted with unique gifts. Spiritual education engages with the big questions of purpose & meaning. It is everything about existence on this planet that is beyond the material.	Is there a governor who is linked to the development of SMSC education? Is there an appointed member of staff who has responsibility for developing SMSC education across the school? Do all staff understand what spiritual education is & how to deliver it? What is the impact of the school's spiritual education on the children's & young people's learning & engagement with higher-order thinking & questioning across the curriculum? Is there appropriate & effective provision for in-service training for teaching & support staff? Is it planned into the teaching & learning for all of the children & young people? Is there evidence of this planning? How is it monitored, assessed & evaluated? What supportive actions or decisions do governors need to make to develop this area further?

Defining & evaluating SMSC education		
Title area	**Definition**	**Evidence – where & what to look for**
Moral	Because of what we believe about the purpose & meaning of life we live by principles & codes that guide our choices between right & wrong.	Is there effective & regular in-service training provided for staff & governors, to ensure professional confidence & competency in the delivery of moral education?
	Key points:	What is the impact of moral education on the children's & young people's learning & engagement with moral issues across the curriculum?
	• Because we are all the children of God this influences our moral choices.	
	• We should not make any decision or take any action that degrades or undermines the humanity in another person.	Is it planned into the teaching & learning for all of the children & young people?
	• Our moral code impacts on our stewardship of the environment & the whole of creation.	Is there evidence of this planning?
		How is it monitored, assessed & evaluated?
		What supportive actions or decisions do governors need to make to develop this area further?

Title area	Definition	Evidence – where & what to look for
Social	Because of our beliefs & values, our way of relating to self must be governed & informed by belief in the sacredness of life at all its stages. *Key points*: • Respect & care for myself. • Respect & care for others. • Ways of interacting socially. These considerations must be guided by our spirituality & morality.	Is there effective & regular in-service training provided for staff & governors, to ensure professional confidence & competency in the delivery of social education? What is the impact of the school's social education on the children's & young people's learning & engagement with social issues across the curriculum? Is it planned into the teaching & learning for all of the children & young people? Is there evidence of this planning? How is it monitored, assessed & evaluated? What supportive actions or decisions do governors need to make to develop this area further?

Defining & evaluating SMSC education		
Title area	**Definition**	**Evidence – where & what to look for**
Cultural	The ways in which we do things which develop over time within communities. *Key points*: • Traditions. • Rites & rituals. • Customs & practices. Culture gives expression to a community's spirituality, morality & social values.	Is there effective & regular in-service training provided for staff & governors, to ensure professional confidence & competency in the delivery of cultural education? What is the impact of the school's cultural education on the children's & young people's learning & engagement with cultural issues across the curriculum? Is it planned into the teaching & learning for all of the children & young people? Is there evidence of this planning? How is it monitored, assessed & evaluated? What supportive actions or decisions do governors need to make to develop this area further?

An innovative exception to the model

In 2013 the Roman Catholic Diocese of Salford published a very interesting inspection schedule which, although developed in a Roman Catholic context, can equally be applied to C in W or C of E schools, and governors may like to consider whether it is appropriate for their particular school.

A Framework for Review, Evaluation and Celebration of our Catholic Schools in the Diocese of Salford,[1] while containing many of the same elements as other dioceses' reviews, at the request of headteachers pushed the concept of review and self-evaluation much further. Drawing on the work of Thomas Groome in his book *Educating for Life: A Spiritual Vision for Every Teacher and Parent*,[2] the diocese categorised their areas for review, self-evaluation and celebration as what commonly became referred to as the "five Ws":

- Word
- Welcome
- Welfare
- Worship
- Witness

The diocesan Office for Education took each of these Ws and used them as a framework for identifying how the questions surrounding the Section 48 inspection had been responded to by each individual school. Governors, heads and teachers were provided with a very detailed analysis of what

to look for in evaluating the effectiveness of each of the Ws. This process provides a deep analysis of each area and clearly highlights both strengths and weaknesses. The framework invites the review and evaluation process to examine each area from the viewpoint of:

- The whole school.
- The curriculum.
- The children's and young people's experience.

Governors and headteachers alike were reported to have found the process both challenging and helpful. Feedback from governors was that they felt it was particularly useful because of its rootedness in the Church's mission in education, while one head observed that, "With this process there is no place to hide!"

As part of the ongoing governor training, governors were invited to attend sessions on how to use the framework, not just for preparing for Ofsted, but as a living, ongoing tool for review, self-evaluation and celebration. To involve as many governors as possible, some governing bodies allocated each of the five Ws to two or three governors to focus on for a year, assisted by a key member of staff. In this way it becomes manageable and governors and staff are engaged together in a constructive process of review and evaluation. If you use this model, it is important to have it as a standing item on the agenda for governors' meetings, so you can hear each team's findings and progress.

Getting the right support for review and self-evaluation

Your first port of call is naturally your diocesan website, where you should find advice and support on a whole range of topics. Look at other dioceses' websites too – there may be material which is not covered in depth in your own diocese.

Governor Mark

Governor Mark is a national award. The kite mark is a very helpful form of external evaluation of the quality of governance in a school, providing a very thorough health check. It is administered by Governance, Leadership and Management (GLM), in partnership with other organisations, to promote and support the National Standards and Governor Mark systems. More and more governing bodies are now using this process. If you are not familiar with it it would be well worth the whole governing body having a look at the Governor Mark Standards document.

Sometimes governors work hard and make a real difference, but no proper record is ever made of this. Governor Mark helps to sharpen practice as well as create the framework through which governor support and challenge can be shown through real evidence.[3]

By undertaking this process you will be able to demonstrate how you are impacting on school improvement and pupil outcomes, and provide evidence of supporting and challenging the school as well as your shared strategic leadership.

Reflection

• Has your governing body carried out a skills audit in order to inform their strengths and areas for development?

• If the audit has been carried out, is everyone clear about what needs to be done and are these steps being taken?

ENDNOTES

[1] Diocese of Salford, *A Framework for Review, Evaluation and Celebration of our Catholic Schools in the Diocese of Salford*: http://cpdf.org.uk/images/uploads/Framework_document.pdf

[2] Thomas Groome, *Educating for Life: A Spiritual Vision for Every Teacher and Parent* (Allen, TX: Thomas More Press, 1998), 203-212.

[3] GLM Quality Mark for School Governance: http://glmpartnership.org/wp-content/uploads/2015/10/GM_revised_document_jan15.pdf

CHAPTER 6
WHEN THE INSPECTOR CALLS:
Preparing for an inspection

School inspections have a reputation for being highly stressful and for distracting school staff and governors alike from the essential jobs of teaching and governance. But whatever you have heard, or whatever your own experience of inspections might be, it is important that there is a central body whose job it is to take an impartial and independent view of what is happening in individual schools in the compulsory sector in England and Wales. Equally, it matters that church schools undergo an additional level of scrutiny, to ensure that the running and management of each one reflects its Christian foundation, ethos and values.

Governors want what is the best for their schools and it is when that the school is due to be inspected that even the most experienced among them can feel vulnerable – not to mention stressed. However, there are many resources to help governors understand what is required and how to provide evidence for the performance of the school – including the National Society, Diocesan Boards of Education (DBES) and external consultants. There are also practical measures, both long- and short-term, that can be taken to ensure that the inspectors are satisfied that the school is performing to the best of its ability and that any necessary improvements are being made from one inspection to the next.

One of the most important measures that can be taken is not an action or policy, but involves adopting a particular outlook and attitude towards the inspection system. If you and the rest of the governing body and staff view inspection as an ongoing process that you are engaged in, rather than a one-off event that is imposed upon you, and introduce a regular and robust system of checks, you will have already much of the information you need in place when an inspection is announced. What's more, you will be better used to review and self-evaluation processes, so it will feel like less of an intrusion into the business of running a school.

Every school must be a living, growing community always striving for excellence, so every school needs to know its next steps, regardless of inspection grade. Although an inspection may seem a daunting process, it is actually something that can provide a framework by which a school can identify and rejoice in its strengths. It also highlights key areas for development or improvement, and so can be a means by which areas of weakness are identified and prompt a plan for improvement.

Chapter Five offers suggestions and resources to help a governing body stay ahead of the game, while in this chapter you will find many more resources that

are specifically applicable to a school that is due to be inspected. Even so, it will do no harm if you as a governing body work through this chapter as a form of ongoing review and self-evaluation, whether or not you are being inspected.

The framework of inspections

All schools in England are subject to Ofsted[1] inspections and all schools in Wales are subject to Estyn[2] inspections, and as a governor you should certainly receive literature and guidance about these. This will surely point out that *all* schools – not just church schools – are evaluated on the way in which they deliver spiritual, moral, social and cultural education (SMSC) throughout the curriculum. However, it's worth underlining here, as this single measure can make a difference to the overall rating given to a school. Even if all other areas are deemed "Outstanding" (in England) or "Excellent" (in Wales), if the SMSC rating is lower (for example "Good", "Satisfactory" or "Adequate"), that will be the final rating given by the inspectors.

SIAMS Section 48 and Gwella Section 50

For a Church of England (C of E) or Church in Wales (C in W) school there are additional inspections, which are carried out with the principal objective of evaluating the distinctiveness and effectiveness of the school *as a church school*:[3]

In England these are known as SIAMS (Statutory Inspection of Anglican and Methodist Schools), or Section 48 (of the [English] Education Act 2005) inspections.[4]

In Wales they are known as Gwella, or Section 50 (of the [Welsh] Education Act 2005) inspections.[5]

Four key questions

In both England and Wales, inspectors will pose four key questions:

- How well does the school, through its distinctive Christian character, meet the needs of all learners?

- What is the impact of collective worship on the school community?

- How effective is the RE?

- How effective are the leadership and management of the school as a church school?[6]

For each of these questions, one of four grades will be given:

- SIAMS: Outstanding, Good, Satisfactory, Inadequate.

- Gwella: Excellent, Good, Adequate, Unsatisfactory.

The rating given will be evidence-based and as objective as possible. Inspectors use a framework and guidance that is nationally agreed and common to all inspections.

Governors can go a long way towards ensuring that when the inspectors arrive, the school, headteacher, other staff and the governors themselves are all equal to the task and able to show the school in the best possible light.

Following are some tips on how to prepare for an inspection:

- Be sure that record-keeping is up to date. Build good relationships with administrative staff and pop into the office when you are passing to have a look at the attendance records.

- Touch base with the head on a regular basis – after all you appointed them and need to know what their particular concerns might be.

- Know what's happening at the "coal face". Are there any particular concerns among parents and pupils? They might not necessarily need addressing on the spot, but keep an eye on any that could develop into a concern for governors over time.

- Ensure that the governing body has a schedule for review and self-evaluation in preparation for inspection.

Just as it is important to be ready in terms of administration, so it is vital to be prepared for the inspection spiritually – both individually and collectively, as a governing body. One way in which this could be achieved is by organising a quiet day for the whole governing body.

Reflection on the performance of the school, using the four key SIAMS and Gwella questions (see previous page) should be at the heart of the work of the governing body. The following is a self-evaluation toolkit used in one diocese in England.[7] It is based on the National Society's Toolkit Form, which guides governors through the process of self-evaluation and inspection.

Self-evaluation toolkit for church schools

It is important that this is used with reference to the National Society's Framework for Inspection and Self-evaluation of Church of England, Methodist and Ecumenical Schools.[8]

	School details
Name of school	
Type of school (primary or secondary)	
Status (VA, VC, Foundation, Academy)	
Local authority	
Diocese	
Number on roll	
School's unique reference number	
Date	

School context

	School context
Name of school	
Date of the last Section 48 inspection	

This is an opportunity for you to provide a few bullet points to explain the context of your school.

You may wish to comment on: school status (including any recent change in status and funding agreement); number on roll (NOR); social and economic circumstances; staffing changes; children and young people with disabilities/learning difficulties, etc.

All the forms and tables in this book can be downloaded from: www.rpdownloads.co.uk/Church-School-Governor-Resources_c_27.html, using the code: GOV001

The vision and values of the school

You may wish to draw upon or include the school mission statement, values statement or school aims as agreed by the school community.

Summary

In about fifty words, please summarise the distinctiveness and effectiveness of your school as a church school.

Progress in addressing the focus for development in the previous inspection	
Schools may wish to add further points as necessary	
Focus for development 1:	
(Relates to core question 1 2 3 4)	
Action taken	**Impact**
Focus for development 2:	
(Relates to core question 1 2 3 4)	
Action taken	**Impact**
Focus for development 3:	
(Relates to core question 1 2 3 4)	
Action taken	**Impact**

How well does the school, through its distinctively Christian character, meet the needs of all its learners?			
Prompts	Provision	Impact of provision	Evidence of impact
1a. How well the Christian character contributes to the academic achievement, personal development & well-being of all learners, regardless of ability or background.			
The impact of the school's Christian character on the achievement of individuals & groups, & the proportion of learners making expected levels of progress, particularly those who are vulnerable. This should be based on national data & the school's current analysis.			
The effectiveness of the school's Christian character in ensuring the highest levels of personal development & well-being.			
How effectively the school promotes good attendance & addresses issues relating to poor attendance & exclusion & how strategies reflect its Christian character.			

Prompts	Provision	Impact of provision	Evidence of impact
Christian values: The extent to which the school's values are distinctively Christian in character, in addition to being shared human values. The extent to which all members of the school community & particularly learners can make links between the values & biblical teaching. The school's effectiveness in ensuring that Christian values make a significant impact on the lives of all members of the school community. The extent to which learners are able to recognise that values are important to those of other faith traditions & those of none.			
1b. How effectively the Christian character supports the SMSC development of all learners, whether they are Christian, of other faiths, or of none.			
The breadth of experiences available to all learners through curricular & extracurricular activities. How well the school offers opportunities for learners to reflect on & respond to beliefs, values & profound human experiences from a range of faith perspectives. The extent to which the opportunities for spiritual development are characterised by distinctive Christian values. How well daily worship, RE & other aspects of the curriculum enable learners to make informed choices based on Christian values. The extent to which the school operates as a distinctively Christian community.			

Prompts	Provision	Impact of provision	Evidence of impact
1c. How effectively the distinctively Christian character shapes the relationships between all members of the school community.			
How well the school fosters positive relationships based on distinctively Christian values between all members of the school community. How well members of the school articulate the link between their behaviour & biblical teaching. How well the school promotes personal self-esteem, good work attitudes & mutual support based upon its distinctively Christian values.			
1d. How well the Christian character promotes an understanding of & respect for diverse communities.			
How well learners understand the role of the Christian Church, particularly the Anglican Communion, at a local, national & international level. How well learners understand Christianity as a multicultural world faith. To what extent learners understand & respect difference & diversity within local, national & global faith communities.			
1e. The contribution of RE to the Christian character of the school.			
The contribution RE makes to the Christian character of the school. The contribution RE makes to learners' SMSC development. How well RE contributes to learners' understanding of & respect for diverse faiths & cultures.			
Identified areas for development:			
			Overall grade: 1 2 3 4

How well does the school through its distinctive Christian character meet the needs of all learners?					
	How well the Christian character contributes to academic achievement, personal development & well-being of all learners, regardless of ability or background	How effectively the Christian character supports the SMSC development of all learners whether they are Christian, of other faiths or of none	How effectively key Christian values shape the relationships between all members of the school community	How well the Christian character promotes an understanding of & respect for diverse communities	The contribution of RE to the Christian character of the school
Outstanding	Distinctively Christian values are made explicit & are deeply embedded in the daily life of the school. All members of the school community articulate the distinctively Christian characteristics of the school's values & the significant impact they have on the daily lives & achievements of learners. The school's Christian character has a high profile & clearly shapes its approach to issues of attendance & pupil exclusion for all groups of learners.	There is a highly developed interpretation of spirituality shared across the school community. Learners have regular opportunities to engage in high-quality experiences that develop a personal spirituality. They are passionate & confident to express their thoughts & views in considerable depth through a rich variety of styles & media. The Christian character & values of the school have a significant impact on the SMSC development of all learners.	The behaviour of learners is of the highest standard & relationships between all members of the school community are consistently attributed to the Christian character & values of the school.	Learners are fully aware that Christianity is a multicultural world faith. They have a high degree of understanding & respect for diversity & difference both within the Church & in other faith communities.	Learners are excited & challenged by RE. It makes a significant contribution to learners' SMSC development & plays a major role in determining the Christian character of the school.

	How well the Christian character contributes to academic achievement, personal development & well-being of all learners, regardless of ability or background	How effectively the Christian character supports the SMSC development of all learners whether they are Christian, of other faiths or of none	How effectively key Christian values shape the relationships between all members of the school community	How well the Christian character promotes an understanding of & respect for diverse communities	The contribution of RE to the Christian character of the schoo
Good	Distinctively Christian values are clearly expressed. This ensures that most members of the school recognise the distinctive characteristics of the school's values & identify how they affect their daily lives & their achievements. The school's Christian character consistently informs its approach to issues of attendance & pupil exclusion for all groups of learners.	The school has a clear definition of spirituality that is understood by most adults. Experiences are identified in the curriculum, which provides opportunities for learners to explore spirituality. Learners respond well & are developing the ability to express their thoughts clearly & with confidence. The Christian character & values of the school contribute to the SMSC development of learners.	Learners behave well & relationships between all members of the school community are generally linked to the Christian character & values of the school.	Learners have some understanding of Christianity as a multicultural world faith & respect the diversity & difference within other faith communities.	Learners readily recognise the importance of RE in their lives. It makes a positive contribution to learners' SMSC development & to the Christian character & values of the school.

	How well the Christian character contributes to academic achievement, personal development & well-being of all learners, regardless of ability or background	How effectively the Christian character supports the SMSC development of all learners whether they are Christian, of other faiths or of none	How effectively key Christian values shape the relationships between all members of the school community	How well the Christian character promotes an understanding of & respect for diverse communities	The contribution of RE to the Christian character of the school
Satisfactory	Most members of the school recognise the school's values as distinctively Christian & acknowledge the difference they make to their daily lives & achievement. The school's Christian character sometimes informs the way in which it approaches issues of attendance & pupil exclusion.	There is some understanding of spirituality among the school's leaders. Opportunities for spiritual development are not always clearly identified in the curriculum or in other areas of school life. Consequently, learners' ability to respond to these experiences is at an early stage of development. The Christian character & values of the school have a limited impact on the SMSC development of learners.	The behaviour of learners is mostly good & relationships between all members of the school community are generally attributed to the Christian character & values of the school.	Learners have only a basic awareness of Christianity as a multicultural world faith & this restricts their understanding of & respect for diversity within the Church.	Learners have generally favourable views of RE & acknowledge its importance in their lives. RE contributes, although inconsistently, to learners' SMSC development & to the Christian character of the school.
Inadequate	Members of the school community have very little understanding of distinctive Christian values with the consequence that these values make almost no impact on the daily life of the school. The school's approach to pupil attendance & exclusion is not related to its Christian values & is ineffective.	There is no clear understanding of spirituality among the school leaders. The school has little idea of how to provide opportunities for spiritual development. Learners show little enthusiasm to engage & respond to experiences for spiritual development & demonstrate a lack of ability to express their thoughts.	The behaviour of learners is often poor & relationships between some members of the school community fall short of what is expected in a church school.	Learners have little understanding or respect for diversity & difference within the Church & other faith communities.	Learners express mixed or negative views of RE & often fail to see its importance in their lives. RE makes a very limited contribution to learners' SMSC development & to the Christian character of the school.

Within the context of a distinctively Christian character:			
What is the impact of collective worship on the school community?			
Prompts	Provision	Impact of provision	Evidence of impact
The extent to which learners & adults engage with collective worship, its relevance & the way it makes a difference to the lives of members of the whole school community.			
The impact of collective worship & the extent to which it: Is engaging, inspiring & transformational. Informs behaviour, attitudes, relationships & school life. Includes a range of creative opportunities, e.g. music, silence, symbols, drama.			
The extent to which collective worship is distinctively Christian, setting out the values of the school in their Christian context.			
The central attributes of collective worship & the extent to which they: Develop the Christian vision, values & ethos of the school & contribute to the SMSC development of participants. Provide opportunities for participants to gather, engage & respond in a variety of ways, grounded in distinctively Christian teaching. Provide opportunities to understand & celebrate festivals in the Church's year & reflect local Anglican practice, including the Eucharist/Communion where appropriate.			

Prompts	Provision	Impact of provision	Evidence of impact
How well collective worship develops personal spirituality within the school community through a range of experiences, including a focus on prayer.			
The centrality of prayer & reflection & the extent to which: • Learners understand the nature & purpose of prayer & reflection. • Learners understand the part this may play within an individual's life & in the life of the worshipping community. • Prayer contributes to the spiritual development of the whole school community. • Appropriate opportunities are provided for prayer & other worship activities, such as Christian reflection, outside collective worship.			
How well collective worship enables participants to develop an understanding of Jesus Christ & a Christian understanding of God as Father, Son and Holy Spirit.			
The theological basis of collective worship & the extent to which it: • Contributes to learners' understanding of Christian theological concepts & beliefs at an appropriate level. • Reflects the Trinitarian nature of Christianity. • Gives the Bible a significant place in worship.			

Prompts	Provision	Impact of provision	Evidence of impact
How effectively the school community is involved in the planning, leadership & evaluation of collective worship.			
The leadership & management of collective worship & the extent to which: • Learners regularly encounter a range of worship leaders, including learners themselves, who ensure that worship is creative, alive, inclusive & accessible. • Worship is planned systematically so that there is continuity, cohesion, variety & a clear focus on Christian beliefs & festivals. • Planning, monitoring & evaluation involve the whole school community & result in improvement.			

Identified areas for development:

Overall grade: 1 2 3 4

	Within the context of a distinctively Christian character: What is the impact of collective worship on the school community?				
	Impact of worship	Central attributes of worship	Prayer/reflection	Theological basis of worship	Leadership & management of collective worship
Outstanding	Across the school community great value is placed on collective worship. Its place in school life & its impact on individuals are readily & clearly articulated.

Collective worship is inspirational & inclusive. It engages all learners & its impact can be clearly discerned in all aspects of relationships & school life. | Collective worship regularly includes biblical material & Christian teaching, & learners are able to relate this to the school's core values & their own lives.

Learners can identify clearly the distinctive features of different Christian traditions in worship, particularly local Anglican practice, the seasons of the Church's year & Christian festivals.

Themes raise aspirations, inspire a high level of spiritual & moral reflection, & challenge learners to take responsibility for their own conduct & charitable social actions expressed in Christian terms. | Learners understand the value of personal prayer & reflection as part of their own spiritual journey. They seek out opportunities for this in their own lives & contribute confidently & sensitively to prayer in worship. | Collective worship has a strong focus on the person of Jesus Christ & learners understand the central position he occupies in the Christian faith.

Collective worship has a strong focus on God as Father, Son and Holy Spirit. Learners recognise this & talk about it with an impressive degree of understanding. | Learners are confident in planning & leading acts of worship, whether prepared beforehand or spontaneous, & have frequent opportunities to do so.

A range of leaders, including staff, clergy & representatives from different Christian traditions, together with a variety of settings for acts of worship, offer learners a rich experience of worship. |

	Impact of worship	Central attributes of worship	Prayer/reflection	Theological basis of worship	Leadership & management of collective worship
Good	Members of the school community see the importance of worship in the life of the school & are able to talk about what it means to them. Learners recognise the value of worship, respond positively & participate willingly. There is evidence of the impact of collective worship on all aspects of school life, including attitudes, behaviour & relationships.	Collective worship often includes biblical material & learners are able to make some links between this & their own lives & to the school's core values. Learners have an understanding of different Christian traditions in worship, particularly local Anglican practice, the seasons of the Church's year & Christian festivals, although they cannot always articulate these fully. Themes are relevant & pay close attention to learners' spiritual & moral development. In response, learners take some action in the service of others.	Learners understand the purpose of prayer & reflection in both formal & informal contexts. Many make use of prayer in their own lives & regularly contribute relevant & appropriate prayers to school worship.	Collective worship often includes teaching about the person of Jesus Christ & learners have an understanding of his important place in worship. Learners are aware of God as Father, Son and Holy Spirit in worship & are able to talk about this with some measure of understanding.	Learners enjoy contributing within collective worship & are increasingly taking responsibility for particular aspects. Staff & clergy are regularly involved in planning the collective worship programme & leading worship in a range of settings, with some involvement of other Christian traditions.

	Impact of worship	Central attributes of worship	Prayer/reflection	Theological basis of worship	Leadership & management of collective worship
Satisfactory	Collective worship is recognised as important in the life of the school community & is said to be valued. There is limited but growing evidence of the impact of collective worship on the wider lives of members of the school community.	Collective worship sometimes includes biblical material but its relation to learners' lives & the school's core values is not always explicit. Learners have some understanding of a few different Christian traditions in worship, mainly related to local Anglican practice & to some Christian festivals. Themes support the school's core values, particularly in the area of moral development. Spiritual development may be more limited because planning for this is less focused. Occasionally learners are prompted to respond in service to others.	Learners experience opportunities for prayer but there is limited understanding of its value & relevance to everyday life.	Learners have some knowledge of the life of Jesus Christ though his significance in worship is not fully understood. Reference is made to God as Father, Son and Holy Spirit on occasions, but the significance of this has not been made explicit to learners.	Learners behave well in worship, are attentive & respond to the different elements. However, they are often passive & do not yet take responsibility for aspects of worship. Planning provides a basic structure for collective worship, but insufficient consideration is given to the coherent development of Christian themes. The main Christian festivals are usually included. Responsibility for planning lies with a few members of staff with little involvement from other members of the school community. There is limited variation in the pattern & setting for collective worship.

	Impact of worship	Central attributes of worship	Prayer/reflection	Theological basis of worship	Leadership & management of collective worship
Inadequate	Learners show at best half-hearted or little response to aspects of worship, which does not hold a distinctive place in the daily life of the school, & learners cannot see its importance in their lives.	Learners have limited awareness of different Christian traditions, including Anglican practice. The major Christian festivals are celebrated but learners gain little understanding of Christian beliefs & values from worship. There is little to raise learners' spiritual awareness or to directly inspire them in the service of others.	Prayer & reflection play a limited role in the pattern of school life, so learners derive little spiritual benefit.	Neither the place in history of the person of Jesus Christ, nor biblical material are given prominence in worship & its key elements have a low profile. As a result learners are frequently not engaged in worship.	Little monitoring & evaluation of worship occurs & no account is taken of learners' views.

Within the context of a distinctively Christian character:			
How effective is the RE? (To be specifically inspected in VA schools only)			
Prompts	Provision	Impact of provision	Evidence of impact
3a. The achievement of learners in RE.			
Progress & standards based upon the school's performance data: • Standards attained by learners at the end of each Key Stage. • Progress for individuals & groups of learners, considering their starting points. • How well gaps in performance are narrowing for different groups of learners (where information is available).			
3b. The quality of teaching & learning in RE.			
Quality of teaching & learning: • Teachers' understanding & implementation of high-quality RE teaching over time, based on observation of lessons, the school's own monitoring, other learning activities, discussion with learners & scrutiny of their work. • The extent to which learning activities address the attainment targets & enable learners to acquire & apply the skills set out in the RE syllabus. • The extent to which RE makes a contribution to the distinctively Christian values of the school & to the SMSC development of learners. • The extent to which learners enjoy RE & are enabled to speak about religious ideas & faith.			

Prompts	Provision	Impact of provision	Evidence of impact
3c. The effectiveness of the curriculum in RE & especially the teaching of Christianity.			
Quality of the curriculum: • The extent to which the schools meets the National Society *Statement of Entitlement for Religious Education,*[9] & in particular, whether Christianity is the majority study: - Key Stages 1-3, at least 2/3 Christianity. - Key Stage 4, the study of Christianity will be a significant & substantial part of any public qualification. - Key Stage 5, the opportunity for the study of Christianity at AS & A level. • The RE provision for all students in the sixth form. • The proportion of curriculum time dedicated to meeting RE objectives (5%-10%). • The extent to which pupil achievement in RE is equal or better than comparable subjects. • The proportion of learners taking a recognised & appropriate qualification at Key Stage 4.			

Prompts	Provision	Impact of provision	Evidence of impact
3d. The effectiveness of the leadership & management of RE.			
The extent to which monitoring of the quality of teaching, learning & assessment leads to an improvement in the performance of learners across the school. The extent to which RE works with & informs effective teaching & learning across the curriculum.			
Identified areas for development:			

Overall grade: 1 2 3 4

Within the context of a distinctively Christian character:			
How effective is RE?			
	The achievement of learners in RE	**The quality of teaching & learning in RE**	**The effectiveness of the curriculum in RE & especially the teaching of Christianity**	**The effectiveness of the leadership & management**
Outstanding	Standards of attainment of all learners are in line with national expectations, with a significant number attaining higher than the national average. Attainment is high & progress is rapid in developing an understanding of Christianity & a broad range of religious beliefs. In exceptional circumstances, where groups of learners attain below those nationally, the gap is narrowing dramatically over a period of time as shown by attainment data.	Learners are inspired by the subject & learn exceptionally well. They develop & apply a wide range of higher-level skills to great effect in their enquiry, analysis, interpretation, evaluation & reflection of their understanding of the impact of religion on believers. Learners are impressive in the way that they use creativity & originality to apply their knowledge & skills in RE to their own personal reflections on questions of meaning & purpose. The majority of teaching is outstanding & never less than consistently good. Highly effective use of assessment informs teaching & learning in RE & exemplar evidence demonstrates progress made by learners.	RE has a very high profile within the school curriculum & learning activities provide fully for the needs of all learners. The RE curriculum is rich & varied, enabling learners to acquire a thorough knowledge & understanding of the Christian faith through a wide range of learning opportunities. The RE curriculum provides opportunities for learners to understand & make links between the beliefs, practices & value systems of the range of faiths studied. Links with the Christian values of the school & SMSC development are intrinsic to the RE curriculum & have a significant impact on learners.	Rigorous & extensive monitoring & evaluation results in well-focused action plans that demonstrably lead to improvement. Subject leadership has the highest level of subject expertise & the vision to realise ambitious expectations & improvement.

	The achievement of learners in RE	The quality of teaching & learning in RE	The effectiveness of the curriculum in RE & especially the teaching of Christianity	The effectiveness of the leadership & management
Good	Standards of attainment for the large majority of learners are at least in line with national expectations & often higher. Learners make good progress given their starting points. Or, standards of attainment are average but learners make rapid & sustained progress given their starting points over a period of time. In exceptional circumstances overall attainment may be slightly lower than national expectations, but with some groups of learners making outstanding progress.	Learners understand the value of the subject & they mostly learn well. They develop a range of skills, including some of the following: enquiry, analysis & interpretation, evaluation & reflection. Learners have a good ability to apply these skills to understanding the impact of religion on believers. Learners show originality & creativity in applying their knowledge & skills in RE & are developing the ability to apply this to questions of meaning & purpose. The majority of teaching is good. Assessment procedures are in place & these inform planning, teaching & learning.	RE has a high profile within the school curriculum & learning activities are differentiated to meet the needs of different groups of learners. Learners display a secure knowledge of many of the key aspects of Christianity & the Bible & the main practices & beliefs of the other faiths & cultures studied. RE makes a good contribution to the Christian values of the school & to the learners' SMSC development.	Effective use is made of a range of routine monitoring & evaluation procedures that accurately identify strengths & focus on raising standards that lead to improvement in pupil performance. The subject leader effectively communicates expectations to senior leaders, governors & staff about improvement in teaching & learning in RE & is well informed on current developments in RE.

	The achievement of learners in RE	The quality of teaching & learning in RE	The effectiveness of the curriculum in RE & especially the teaching of Christianity	The effectiveness of the leadership & management
Satisfactory	Standards of attainment for the majority of learners are in line with national expectations. Progress is satisfactory, with learners making at least comparable progress to national expectations. Or, attainment is low but there is accurate & convincing evidence that progress over a sustained period of time is improving strongly & securely. The quality of learning & engagement within the subject is generally good but with some variation in some year groups or Key Stages.	Teachers sometimes, though not always, ensure that lessons are structured around the development of skills such as enquiry & reflection. Learners have a satisfactory knowledge & understanding of Christianity & some religions & beliefs, but their ability to answer questions of meaning & purpose is limited. The majority of teaching is satisfactory & there is likely to be some good teaching. The RE curriculum caters for the learning needs of some learners, but those needing either reinforcement or more challenging learning activities are not routinely planned for. Some assessment takes place, but this is inconsistent across year groups & does not always accurately inform future teaching & learning.	The RE curriculum offers some opportunities to enhance the SMSC development of learners. The RE curriculum offers learners some opportunities to understand the main teachings, beliefs & practices of Christianity & some other world faiths, but implementation is inconsistent & is therefore not fully effective. As a result, learners do not have sufficient knowledge or understanding of religions nor of respect between diverse faith communities. RE has modest links to some aspects of the school's Christian values, but these are not made explicit & are not consistently identified in teachers' planning.	There is regular monitoring of some aspects of RE, & self-evaluation is broadly accurate in identifying priorities for improvement that offer adequate challenge. The subject leader is aware of current developments in RE & incorporates some of these in his/her practice.

	The achievement of learners in RE	The quality of teaching & learning in RE	The effectiveness of the curriculum in RE & especially the teaching of Christianity	The effectiveness of the leadership & management
Inadequate	Standards of teaching, learning & assessment are inadequate, with the result that standards of attainment & rates of progress for the majority of learners & groups of learners are consistently lower than national expectations.	The RE curriculum makes little contribution to the Christian values of the school & its promotion of SMSC development is limited.	Insufficient opportunities exist to develop learners' knowledge & understanding of Christianity or other faiths & the impact on the lives of believers.	Subject leadership is poor. Procedures for the monitoring & evaluation of RE are weak & fail to identify essential improvements in teaching & learning.

Within the context of a distinctively Christian character:			
How effective are the leadership & management of the school as a church school?			
Prompts	Provision	Impact of provision	Evidence of impact
4a. The extent to which leaders articulate an explicit Christian vision that has an impact on: **Standards of achievement; the distinctively Christian character of the school; the well-being of all the whole school community.**			
How well an explicit Christian vision is articulated & implemented. The impact of the Christian vision on the achievement of all learners including the effectiveness of leaders in helping learners to overcome educational, social & economic disadvantage. How well leaders promote the well-being of all learners, particularly their SMSC development, through a broad & distinctive curriculum in addition to worship & RE.			

Prompts	Provision	Impact of provision	Evidence of impact
4b. The extent to which school leaders secure the impact of this vision through evaluation & strategic planning.			
The impact of monitoring & evaluation on the school's Christian character.

How well governors hold leaders to account for the school's effectiveness as a church school.

The extent to which leaders enable all members of the school community to contribute to & understand the development & implementation of the school's distinctively Christian vision.

The implementation & effectiveness of improvement plans related to the distinctive Christian characteristics of the school.

The extent to which the issues in "Focus for development" from the last inspection have been addressed & in a manner that has brought about positive outcomes for the learners. | | | |

Prompts	Provision	Impact of provision	Evidence of impact
4c. How well leaders prepare for the future leadership across church schools.			
The effectiveness of professional development in enhancing the Christian character of the school. The effectiveness of preparation for the future leadership of church schools by the implementation of an appropriate programme of staff development.			
4d. The effectiveness of partnerships with the local church, the deaneries, the diocese & the wider community, including parents & carers.			
The extent to which leaders & managers form partnerships & engage with the Church in parish, diocesan, national & global communities in a way that enriches the lives of learners. The effectiveness of the incumbent/minister/chaplain/youth worker in supporting individuals & developing the distinctive Christian character of the school. The effectiveness of parental engagement & contribution to school life.			

Prompts	Provision	Impact of provision	Evidence of impact
4e. If the arrangements for RE & collective worship meet statutory requirements.			
The extent to which the National Society Statement of Entitlement for Religious Education[10] *is implemented, in particular:* • Priority given to staff expertise & specialist qualifications in RE. • Priority given to professional development in RE. • The level of resourcing for RE.			
Identified areas for development:			

Overall grade: 1 2 3 4

	Within the context of a distinctively Christian character: How effective are the leadership & management of the school as a church school?				
	The extent to which leaders articulate an explicitly Christian vision that has an impact on: **Standards of achievement; the distinctively Christian character of the school; the well-being of all the whole school community.**	The extent to which school leaders secure the impact of this vision through evaluation & strategic planning.	How well leaders prepare for future leadership across church schools.	The effectiveness of partnerships with the local church, the deaneries, the diocese & the wider community, including the parents & carers.	If the arrangements for RE & collective worship meet statutory requirements.
Outstanding	Leaders have a thorough understanding of the school's performance & distinctiveness based on effective & insightful self-evaluation. Leaders ensure that the whole curriculum is informed by a distinctive Christian vision that contributes well to pupil behaviour & attitudes as well as their SMSC development. Self-evaluation involves all groups in the school community. It leads directly & convincingly to effective strategies for improvement & maintains a strong focus on meeting the needs of all learners.	Leaders consistently & confidently articulate, live out & promote a vision rooted in distinctively Christian values. Leaders readily articulate the impact of explicit Christian values on the lives of learners & on the whole life of the school.	The development of all staff & governors as leaders in church schools is planned strategically with substantial benefits for the current leadership of the school.	Parents, the local church, the diocese & the wider community contribute fully to school life so that there is mutual & substantial benefit for all groups, including their understanding of local, national & global communities.	The leadership of worship & RE is given a high priority & this leads to highly effective practice in both areas.

	The extent to which leaders articulate an explicitly Christian vision that has an impact on: Standards of achievement; the distinctively Christian character of the school; the well-being of all the whole school community.	The extent to which school leaders secure the impact of this vision through evaluation & strategic planning.	How well leaders prepare for future leadership across church schools.	The effectiveness of partnerships with the local church, the deaneries, the diocese & the wider community, including the parents & carers.	If the arrangements for RE & collective worship meet statutory requirements.
Good	Leaders have a good understanding of the school's performance & distinctiveness based on the school's self-evaluation strategies. Leaders ensure that collective worship, RE, & aspects of the curriculum are informed by distinctive Christian values that contribute to learners' good behaviour & attitudes, together with their SMSC development. Self-evaluation strategies lead directly to the school's improvement planning. As a result, achievement & distinctiveness have improved, or previous good performance has been consolidated for all groups of learners.	Leaders articulate & promote a vision based on distinctively Christian values. Leaders clearly describe the impact of Christian values on the learners & on the whole life of the school.	Effective use is made of opportunities that arise for the development of staff & governors as leaders in church schools, with clear benefits for the current leaders.	Parents, the local church, the diocese & the wider community contribute fully to school life in such a way that there are clear benefits for learners, including their understanding of local, national & global communities.	The leaders of worship & RE are given good support in fulfilling their roles & this has enabled them to bring about improvements or maintain the previous good practice.

		Within the context of a distinctively Christian character:			
		How effective are the leadership & management of the school as a church school?			
		The extent to which leaders articulate an explicitly Christian vision that has an impact on: **Standards of achievement; the distinctively Christian character of the school; the well-being of all the whole school community.**	The extent to which school leaders secure the impact of this vision through evaluation & strategic planning.	How well leaders prepare for future leadership across church schools.	The effectiveness of partnerships with the local church, the deaneries, the diocese & the wider community, including the parents & carers.	If the arrangements for RE & collective worship meet statutory requirements.
Satisfactory	Leaders articulate the school's priorities as a church school, although the links between this & the school's self-evaluation are not always understood & do not always lead to improvement. Consequently, not all learners progress as well as they might & the school's distinctive character is not fully developed. Worship, RE & other aspects of the curriculum are based upon Christian values, but these values are present at an implicit rather than an explicit level. As a result, whilst learners recognise the school as a church school, they are not always able to recognise the impact that this has on their SMSC development & well-being.	• Leaders provide a concerted approach to the distinctiveness & effectiveness of the school as a church school, although this is not driven by a clearly developed Christian vision. • Leaders have some awareness of the impact of distinctively Christian values on some aspects of school life, although they are not clear about the difference they make across the whole school community.	The school provides some opportunities for the identification & development of staff & governors as leaders of church schools.	Parents, the church, the diocese & the wider community contribute to school life but this is not always on a regular or sustained basis & this limits the benefit to learners & their understanding of local, national & global communities.	The improvement strategies adopted by the leaders of worship & RE, whilst having some positive impact, are not sufficiently rigorous to bring about sustained improvement.

	The extent to which leaders articulate an explicitly Christian vision that has an impact on: **Standards of achievement; the distinctively Christian character of the school; the well-being of all the whole school community.**	The extent to which school leaders secure the impact of this vision through evaluation & strategic planning.	How well leaders prepare for future leadership across church schools.	The effectiveness of partnerships with the local church, the deaneries, the diocese & the wider community, including the parents & carers.	If the arrangements for RE & collective worship meet statutory requirements.
Inadequate	Self-evaluation strategies are insufficiently rigorous to bring about improvements in pupil achievement, well-being or SMSC development.	One or more of the aspects from "Focus for development" in the last inspection report have not been addressed in a way that has brought about improvement. Leaders & managers do not have a coherent vision or strategic plan for the distinctiveness & effectiveness of the school as a church school.		The school's relationships with the diocese, church, parents & the wider community are weak & make little impact on learners' understanding of local, national & global communities.	The leadership of the school does not ensure that worship or RE have sufficiently high profile in the school. As result both are no better than satisfactory & show little sign of improvement. Arrangements for RE & collective worship may not meet statutory requirements.

From the evidence in the self-evaluation toolkit, please complete these three boxes:
Summary judgement:
Areas in which the school feels it does well:
Areas which the school feels it should develop further:

ENDNOTES

[1] Ofsted: www.gov.uk/government/organisations/ofsted

[2] Estyn: www.estyn.gov.wales

[3] The Church of England/Education & National Society/Church Schools and Academies: www.churchofengland.org

[4] The Archbishops' Council, the National Society & the Methodist Church, *Statutory Inspection of Anglican and Methodist Schools (SIAMS): A Framework for Inspection and Self-evaluation of Church of England and Methodist Schools*: www.churchofengland.org

[5] Church Schools Cymru/Inspection: www.churchschoolscymru.org

[6] The Archbishops' Council, the National Society & the Methodist Church, *Statutory Inspection of Anglican and Methodist Schools (SIAMS)*: www.churchofengland.org

[7] The Diocese of Oxford/Schools/Siams: www.oxford.anglican.org

[8] The Archbishops' Council, the National Society & the Methodist Church, *Statutory Inspection of Anglican and Methodist Schools (SIAMS)*: www.churchofengland.org

[9] This is a statement from the National Society, setting out the way in which religious education should be taught in C of E and C in W schools.
The Archbishops' Council Education Division & the National Society, *Religious Education in Church of England Schools: A Statement of Entitlement from the Board of Education/National Society Council* (n.d.): www.churchofengland.org

[10] Ibid.

Modern Stained Glass, *The Call of the First Disciples*

CHAPTER 7

PRAYERS AND PRAYING TOGETHER

Time to pray

This chapter is designed as a resource to help develop the prayer life of a governing body and the individual governors. Often governor meeting agendas are very full and it is natural to want to get on with the business at hand. But that is all the more reason for governors – believers and non-believers alike – to take a few moments at the beginning of each meeting to pause and come together as a centred group, focusing on the meeting ahead and putting aside other preoccupations. Similarly, at the end of a meeting, a short prayer consolidates and strengthens any decisions that have been made.

Governing bodies should include "Opening prayers" as the first item on the agenda, always understanding and appreciating that some of the governors may not be Christians. Many non-Christians are happy to share in a time of prayer even if they do not subscribe to the sentiments expressed, although others may be less comfortable. One compromise, if it is expected that all governors, whether of any faith or none, attend the opening prayers, is that the leader introduces the prayers with a statement along the lines of: "If you do not wish to pray, please use the time to reflect on the work we are about to do and the wider concerns of this school." If a substantial proportion of the school community belongs to another faith (as is the case in many inner-city church schools), it may be appropriate to include a prayer from another faith community, for example the traditional Jewish Sabbath prayer over children from the Old Testament (Numbers 6:24-26):

> The Lord bless you and keep you;
> the Lord make his face to shine upon you, and be gracious to you;
> the Lord lift up his countenance upon you, and give you peace.

> Ye'varech'echa Adonoy ve'yish'merecha.
> Ya'ir Adonoy panav eilecha viy-chuneka.
> Yisa Adonoy panav eilecha, ve'yasim lecha shalom.[1]

Or the Muslim prayer:

> O my Lord, dispose me that I may be thankful for Thy blessing with which Thou hast blessed me and
> my father and mother and that I may do righteousness,
> well-pleasing to Thee and make me righteous also in my seed, surely I turn to Thee and surely I am of those who submit.[2]

Prayer takes place in the heart, not in the head.

Carlo Carretto [3]

What should prayers consist of?

One model for opening prayers is that recommended by Prebendary Sam Wells in his guide to leading public prayers.[4] This examines the "time-honoured shape", or archetypal prayer in the Anglican tradition – the collect. A well-known example is the Collect for Purity, which has five elements:

1. The address to God – "Almighty God", "God the healer".

2. The context in which God has been active and an explanation of why the person praying (on behalf of all those present) believes that God will listen and respond.

3. What precisely what it is that those praying want God to do.

4. The outcome in terms of the change to the community.

5. The conclusion, shaping the prayer in light of the invocation of the Trinity.

So a prayer at the beginning of a governors' meeting following this pattern may be something along the following lines:

God who protects and teaches,
Who gave a practical example of teaching
   through the parables,
Guide and strengthen us as governors,
That we may always act in the best interests
   of all for whom we are responsible.
Through Jesus Christ our Lord, who lives
   and reigns with you in the unity of the Holy
   Spirit, one God, now and for ever.
Amen.

An intercessory prayer can be responsorial – having a petition such as "Lord, in your mercy" responded to with "Hear our prayer".

Meetings might end with a well-known and trusted prayer, such as the Lord's Prayer or the Grace.

Who should lead the prayers?

As with collective worship (see Chapter Four) it is not always the headteacher or Chair of Governors who may be best placed to lead prayers. There may be a governor who has particular skills in this area, or who has particular responsibility for this. Another approach may be to rotate the responsibility, while a third may be to have a group of governors whose responsibility is to plan and lead opening prayers.

Prayers should be as inclusive as possible, but it is probably best to avoid practices that people might disagree on or feel uncomfortable about – such as looking around at the group during the saying of the Grace, or holding hands.

Prayers for governors on different occasions

A prayer for the start of the school year

God of love and mercy, we praise you for the wonder of our being, for all that you have created us to be.

Guide us, governors, staff and children as we begin a new school year.

Bless each one with your strength and grace as we grow in wisdom and knowledge, searching to understand the mystery and wonder of your creation.

We ask this through Jesus Christ our Lord.

Amen.

Governors' prayer for the new school year

All: Come, Holy Spirit!

Come into our school at the start of the year.

Come Holy Spirit, enlighten our minds to your work

… in us;

… through us;

… for us.

May we all become the channel of your love for our community.

All: Come, Holy Spirit!

Help us to be people of courage

… to challenge;

… to change;

… to transform.

So that we may be renewed in our commitment to build the kingdom of God.

All: Come, Holy Spirit!

Come into our gathering at the start of this school year.

Come, Holy Spirit, and open our hearts to you speaking

… in our fellow governors;

… through our children;

… in our teachers and staff.

Inspire us to be a people of hope.

All: Come, Holy Spirit!

Enlighten the eyes of our minds

… to see you in people who challenge us;

… to your working in situations we don't understand;

… to your moving gently in our hearts.

Help us to be a people of wisdom.

Amen.

A prayer for willingness to serve others
(by St Francis of Assisi)

Lord, make us instruments of your peace.
Where there is hatred, let us sow love;
where there is injury, pardon;
where there is discord, union;
where there is doubt, faith;
where there is despair, hope;
where there is darkness, light;
where there is sadness, joy.
Grant that we may not so much seek
to be consoled as to console;
to be understood as to understand;
to be loved as to love.
For it is in giving that we receive;
it is in pardoning that we are pardoned;
and it is in dying that we are born to eternal life.
Amen.

A prayer for children
Loving God,
your Son told his disciples
to become like little children.
Lead us to work for the welfare
and protection of all young people.
May we respect their dignity
that they may flourish in life,
following the example of the same
Jesus Christ our Lord.
Amen.[5]

A prayer before appointing a new headteacher

Father, you have entrusted us with the care of your children here in [Name of school].
Help and guide our minds and hearts today to recognise the person you know we need to lead our school on the next part of its journey.
A journey in loving.
A journey in learning.
A journey in understanding.
A journey in becoming.
A journey in discovery.
A journey in hope.
Open our hearts to hear and our minds to recognise your voice today.
Amen.

A prayer before appointing a new member of staff

Guide us, Lord Jesus, as we greet each candidate today.
May they feel secure and valued.
Inspire each one to share with us their hopes and dreams for the children.
Together help us to discover if this is to be where they should be.
Enlighten our minds with your Holy Spirit so that we may discover their gifts and talents.
May each one feel that they have given of their best.
Amen.

A prayer before the inspector calls

Lord Jesus, fill each one here in our school with your spirit of wisdom and understanding.

Guide us in our answering.

Direct our questioning.

Lighten our worrying.

Strengthen our courage.

Enrich our teaching.

Steady our nerves.

Ignite our passion.

Gentle our speech.

Hold us in the palm of your hand.

Above all let us never forget that this is your work that we do. Be with us today so that we may be ever more true to our calling as teachers of your children, our brothers and sisters.

Amen.

A prayer for our children before SATs

Father of all our children, enlighten and encourage each child here today as they do their tests. We bless you for each one and thank you for the gift that they are for us. May they be able to recall all that you have helped us to teach them and feel proud of their achievements.

Amen.

A prayer before our pupils sit their final examinations

O God, help our students as they sit their examinations,

to recall the things which they have learned and studied.

May they remember clearly and set down that which they know so well.

Steady their nerves and calm their minds,

doing justice for all their hard work.

May each one feel that they have achieved the very best they can.

Amen.

Love to pray – feel the need to pray often through the day and take the trouble to pray. If you want to pray better, you must pray more. Prayer enlarges the heart until it is capable of containing God's gift of himself. Ask and seek and your heart will grow big enough to receive him and keep him as your own.

Mother Teresa[6]

A prayer for the end of term

Christ, our Teacher,

bless everyone in our school

as we come to the end of the year.

Pour out your loving grace

on all who have given so much,

asking only that each one may receive

that which you have prepared for them.

We give thanks for everyone in the school

for this year of nurturing and growth,

of laughter, of fun, of joy of discovery.

We give thanks for the challenges and achievements,

for the hard times, the misunderstandings and the joy
   of forgiveness.

Stay with us in our rest days

so that we may be renewed and restored.

Keep each one safe in your loving embrace

so that we may return renewed to continue

the ongoing discovery of your love.

Amen.

Prayer in times of trouble (attributed to an
unknown Confederate soldier)

I asked for strength that I might achieve;

I was made weak that I might learn humbly to obey.

I asked for health that I might do greater things;

I was given infirmity that I might do better things.

I asked for riches that I might be happy;

I was given poverty that I might be wise.

I asked for power that I might have the praise of men;

I was given weakness that I might feel the need of
   God.

I asked for all things that I might enjoy life;

I was given life that I might enjoy all things.

I got nothing that I had asked for,

but everything that I had hoped for.

Almost despite myself my unspoken prayers were
   answered;

I am, among all men, most richly blessed.

Amen.

Do not forget to say your prayers. If your
prayer is sincere, there will be every time you
pray a new feeling containing an idea in it, an
idea you did not know before, which will give
fresh courage: you will then understand that
prayer is education.

Fyodor Dostoevsky

A prayer for times of rejoicing (Psalm 95:1-7)

O come, let us sing to the Lord;

let us make a joyful noise to the rock of our salvation!

Let us come into his presence with thanksgiving;

let us make a joyful noise to him

with songs of praise!

For the Lord is a great God, and a great King above

all gods.

In his hand are the depths of the earth; the heights of

the mountains are his also.

The sea is his, for he made it, and the dry land, which

his hands have formed.

O come, let us worship and bow down, let us kneel

before the Lord, our Maker!

For he is our God, and we are the people of his

pasture, and the sheep of his hand.

Amen.

A Welsh-language prayer

Gweddi Dydd Gŵyl Dewi

Diolch, diolch am Gymru, diolch am wlad, am dir, am
iaith.

Diolch, diolch am Iesu, am ei gariad, am ei waith;

dyma weddi Dydd Gŵyl Dewi, de a gogledd, cenwch
gan:

boed i'r Cymry garu'r Iesu cadwn Gymru'n Gymru
lan.

Amen.

St David's Day prayer

Thank you, thank you for Wales.

Thank you for our country, land and language.

Thank you, thank you for Jesus,

for his love and his work;

this is a St David's Day prayer,

north and south, sing this song:

let us in Wales love Jesus

and keep our country holy.

God will always answer our prayers; but He
will answer them in His way, and His way
will be the way of perfect wisdom and of
perfect love. Often if He answered our
prayers as we at that moment desire, it would
be the worst thing possible for us, for in our
ignorance we often ask for gifts which would
be our ruin.

William Barclay[7]

Reflection

- What place does prayer play in your ministry as a governor?

- As a governing body, how comfortable are you with taking time to prayer together?

- Are there resources which might help the governing body in prayer?

- Are there resources which might help you as an individual in prayer?

- As governors, how do you think you could assist the school community in their understanding and growth in prayer?

ENDNOTES

1 Quoted in Mark Herringshaw, "A Hebrew blessing for children": www.beliefnet.com
2 Surah Al-Ahqaf, verse 15[1].
3 Carlo Carretto, *The Desert in the City* (London: Fount, 1981).
4 Samuel Wells, *Crafting Prayers for Public Worship* (Norwich: Canterbury Press, 2013).
5 The Church of England/Prayers for Children and Families: www.churchofengland.org © The Archbishops' Council. Used by permission.
6 Quoted in *Mother Teresa: In the Silence of the Heart*, edited by Kathryn Spink (Oxford: Isis, 1985).
7 William Barclay, *The Gospel of Matthew* (Edinburgh: St Andrew Press, 1956).

BIBLIOGRAPHY, FURTHER RESOURCES AND USEFUL LINKS

All the forms and tables in this book can be downloaded from: www.rpdownloads.co.uk/Church-School-Governor-Resources_c_27.html, using the code: GOV001

Useful websites

The Association for Christian Teachers (ACT)

www.christian-teachers.org.uk

A wide range of online resources to support Christian teachers and governors in both C of E and C in W schools, and secular schools.

The Church of England Education

www.churchofengland.org/education.aspx

The Church in Wales Schools

www.churchinwales.org.uk/life/schools

Church Schools Cymru

www.churchschoolscymru.org

Estyn

www.estyn.gov.wales

Estyn is led by Her Majesty's Chief Inspector of Education and Training in Wales and inspects quality and standards. Estyn also provides advice and guidance to the Welsh Government on quality and standards in education and training in Wales.

Governance, Leadership and Management (GLM)

www.glmpartnership.org

The organisation managing "Governor Mark", working with partners to promote and support the National Standards and Governor Mark process.

Inspiring Governors

www.inspiringgovernors.org

The Inspiring Governors Alliance is the result of discussions between the Department for Education, the National Governors' Association, NCOGS, CBI, SGOSS and the Education and Employers Taskforce about how to celebrate the valuable role played by school governors, increase the number of governing bodies actively seeking to recruit and develop high-calibre governors with relevant skills and experience, and increase the number of employers supporting staff to volunteer as governors as well as promoting governance as a key learning and development opportunity for staff.

The National College for Teaching and Leadership (NCTL)

www.gov.uk/government/organisations/national-college-for-teaching-and-leadership

An executive agency, sponsored by the Department for Education, NCTL aims to improve the quality of the education and early years workforce and to help schools to help each other improve.

The National Governors' Association (NGA)

www.nga.org.uk

An independent charity that aims to improve the educational standards and well-being of children and young people through supporting and promoting outstanding governance in all state-funded schools, including academies and free schools. The NGA works closely with, and lobbies, government and the major educational bodies to ensure that the views of governors are fully represented in the national arena.

The National Society for Promoting Religious Education

www.christianvalues4schools.co.uk

Established in 1811 by Joshua Watson (see Chapter One) to provide schools for poor children. Today it administers the SIAMS and Gwella church school inspections (see more in Chapter Six).

Ofsted

www.gov.uk/government/organisations/ofsted

The Office for Standards in Education, Children's Services and Skills. Ofsted inspects and regulates services that care for children and young people, and services providing education and skills for learners of all ages.

Prayer resources

Pray for Schools

www.prayforschools.org/resources/group- resources/inspirational-prayers

Encouraging Christians to hold events to increase prayer for schools in their area.

Faith and Worship

www.faithandworship.com/prayers

A personal collection of prayers written by John Birch to be used in private and public worship.

The Franciscans

www.franciscans.org.uk/franciscan-praying/prayers-of-saint-francis

Sacred Space

www.sacredspace.ie

A very useful site which offers a daily time of meditation that is simple yet challenging.

Further reading

Governors' Handbook

www.gov.uk/government/uploads/system/uploads/attachment_data/file/481147/Governance_handbook_November_2015.pdf

R. Gallagher, J. Trenchard & J. John, *This Is Our Faith* (Chawton: Redemptorist Publications, 2001).

A straightforward explanation about the Christian faith, the Church and worship, written from an Anglican perspective. It is often used as a resource for confirmation candidates.